Fascinating tales of Circle City history

AMAZING INDIANAPOLIS

FEATURING

HARRY HOUDINI, THE "WORST FAMILY IN THE WORLD," THE MARMON WASP, AND THE "KING OF COOL"

Ashley Petry

For Merryn.

Welcome to Indianapolis.

Reedy Press

PO Box 5131

St. Louis, MO 63139

reedypress.com

Library of Congress Control Number: 2025936320

ISBN: 9781681065984

Printed in the United States of America

25 26 27 28 29   5 4 3 2 1

Contents

CHAPTER SEVEN

CHAPTER EIGHT

Acknowledgments

First, I must thank the team at Reedy Press for a decade of guidance. On this book, as always, you have shown how much you care about your authors, and your advice has been invaluable. In particular, thank you to Josh Stevens and Barbara Northcott, as well as the team of designers, copy editors, and proofreaders who helped to shape this book.

The Indiana Historical Society provided many images for this book, for which I am grateful. I also owe a debt of gratitude to the historians and journalists of Indianapolis over the years, who have worked so hard to preserve more than 200 years of city history. And a special thank you to the team behind *The Encyclopedia of Indianapolis*, an incredibly comprehensive and valuable resource.

Finally, I am grateful to my friends and family for their support; I am so lucky to love and be loved by all of you. Bonus points to Mom and Sarah, who have helped me with countless book events over the years. To my 13 nieces and nephews, who are the joys of my life, and to Brooke, Michael, and Henry, as always, forever.

Introduction

Amazing Indianapolis is an essential collection of historical fun facts about the Circle City. It includes vivid profiles of famous (and not so famous) residents, captivating tales of true crime, and fascinating local inventions. It also highlights the city's lost industries and surprising celebrity connections. And it contains a whole lot of weirdness.

My previous book, *Indianapolis: An Illustrated Timeline*, is a formal and serious history of the city. During my research for that book, I came across all kinds of interesting and sometimes wacky stories that simply didn't fit in that book. *Amazing Indianapolis* gives me the opportunity to finally share those tales and paint a more colorful picture of the Circle City.

This book has been a joy to write, and from start to finish the words have come easily. One of my favorite chapters is "Overlooked Locals," which features unknown and forgotten Indy residents who deserve more credit than they receive. Bringing their stories to light creates a more complete and balanced history. The tales of true crime in "The Criminal Element" were darker and harder to write, but some of those stories have a funny side, too. And the chapter titled "Pure Weirdness" is, well, exactly that.

As a lifelong Hoosier, it has been my privilege in recent years to write several books about Indianapolis, a city that tends to be overlooked. If you want to explore the city more deeply yourself, check out my books *100 Things to Do in Indianapolis Before You Die* and *Secret Indianapolis: A Guide to the Weird, Wonderful, and Obscure.* The first book is a bucket list of the best and most meaningful Indianapolis experiences, and the second focuses on off-the-beaten-path adventures.

Thank you, reader, for making these books possible.

The beloved Raggedy Ann was invented here in Indianapolis.

Chapter One

Invented Here

A surprising array of inventions call Indianapolis home, from Barbasol shaving cream to Wonder Bread. Raggedy Ann and Raggedy Andy were born here, alongside the homespun characters in the poetry of James Whitcomb Riley and the comics of Kin Hubbard. The first consumer product to contain transistors—a small radio—was developed here, as was the very first rearview mirror in an automobile. Meanwhile, the local Kingan & Co. meatpacking plant was the first company to package sliced bacon. Some local inventions, such as the odd-looking Vajen-Bader Smoke Protector and Eli Lilly's insulin breakthrough, were intended to save lives. Others, like the world's first machine gun, did the opposite. But either way, all of these inventions reflect the creativity and innovation that are possible here in the Circle City.

Courtesy of Perio, Inc.

Barbasol Shaving Cream

The morning routine was forever changed when Frank Shields invented Barbasol, the first shaving cream. Before Shields's innovation, men had to place shaving soap in a mug and work it into a lather with a brush. Ready-to-use shaving cream saved time and effort, and in particular it improved the shaving process for men with thicker beard hair or more sensitive skin.

A native of Seymour, Indiana, Shields attended Franklin College and MIT. After working in corporate laboratories, the chemical engineer moved to Indianapolis in 1913 with a plan to manufacture glue. Instead he invented Barbasol in 1919, calling it "a sanitary beard softener—no brush, no lather, no rub-in." The name comes from *barba*, the Latin word for "beard," and an abbreviation of the word "solution."

Sales of Barbasol took off in the 1920s, thanks in part to celebrity endorsements in the *Saturday Evening Post.* The Great Depression had little effect on the company, because the product was perceived as a necessity. By 1936 the company occupied four buildings at Senate Avenue and Ninth Street, and it employed about 400 people. During World War II, Barbasol became a staple item in US military ration kits, and for a while the company employed 750 people day and night, with "a special shift for housewives."

Courtesy of Perio, Inc.

Shields died in 1946, leaving behind a 30-room English Tudor mansion in Martinsville. He willed it to the state, with the stipulation that it be used for a governor's residence. But the Indiana constitution requires the chief executive to live in the capital city, and the offer was declined. The estate instead became a game preserve, and later a housing development with the mansion as its clubhouse.

Originally, Barbasol was a thick cream that came in a tube, like toothpaste. In the 1950s, the company switched to a light, fluffy foam that came in aerosolized containers. Despite that innovation—or perhaps because of it—in 1962 the company was purchased by Pfizer, which moved manufacturing operations to New Jersey.

Wonder Bread

In the spring of 1921, mysterious advertisements appeared in Indianapolis newspapers. They promoted a new product called Wonder, but they didn't specify what the product actually was. The city was abuzz until May 21, when the *Indianapolis News* carried the answer. "So now the mystery we will end, / And to every home a message send," read a poem in the advertisement. The product was Wonder Bread, the "bigger, better Taggart loaf."

The Taggart Baking Company was founded in Indianapolis in 1869, and by the turn of the century it was the largest bread bakery in the state, producing more than 300,000 loaves per week. At one time it had nine retail stores in the Indianapolis area, two with attached cafés. Wonder Bread was different from Taggart's previous products because it weighed 1.5 pounds, larger than the standard 1-pound loaf. The loaf was made "with milk, and plenty of it," the ads claimed, and unlike other breads it didn't crumble or dry out when sliced.

Elmer Cline, Taggart's vice president of merchandising development, had been assigned the task of naming the new product. He was stumped until he attended a hot-air-balloon race at the Indianapolis Motor Speedway, where he was filled with wonder by the "kaleidoscope of color." He seized on the word *wonder*. To this day, the colorful dots on Wonder Bread packaging represent those hot-air balloons.

"You will learn to know it by its many colored balloons," one advertisement read, "dedicated to the children of every family, whose health this wonder loaf is designed to protect and build up, by the doctrine of simple, wholesome living."

An early balloon race at the Indianapolis Motor Speedway.

Taggart was purchased by the Continental Baking Company in 1925, giving Wonder Bread a national platform. In the 1930s, it became the first major brand to package sliced bread. It has remained a staple of the American diet for more than a century.

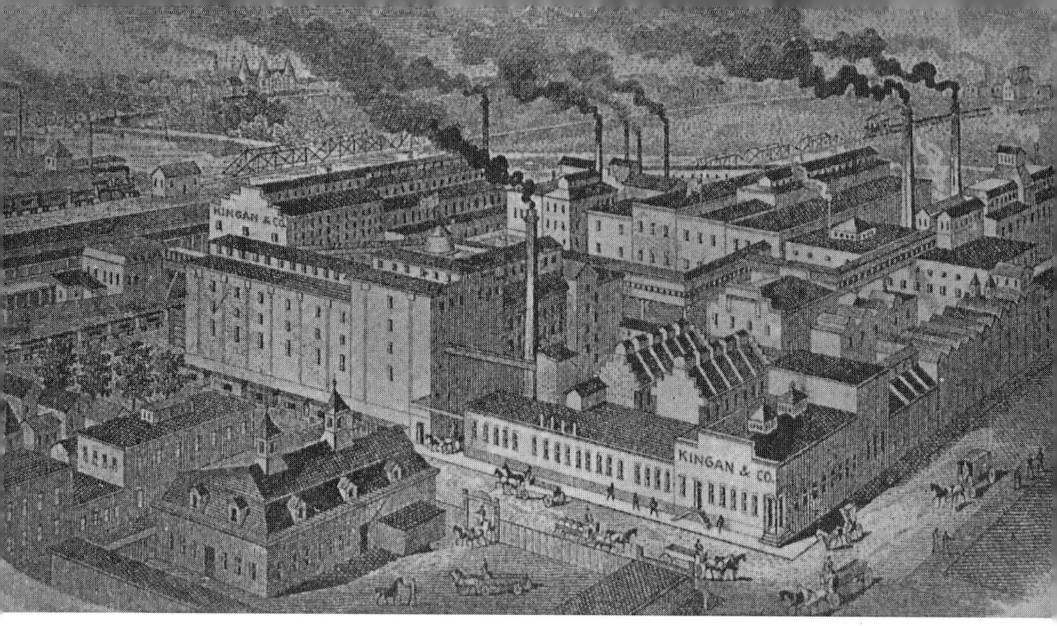

Sliced Bacon

In addition to Wonder Bread, Indianapolis can lay claim to another essential component of the classic BLT. In 1914, Kingan & Co. of Indianapolis became the first company to manufacture packaged sliced bacon.

Built in 1864, the Kingan & Co. pork packing house in Indianapolis was one of the largest of its kind in the world. "This introduction . . . proved to be an epoch in [the city's] growth and development," read *Hyman's Hand Book of Indianapolis* in 1897. By then, the facility spread across 15 acres, employed about 1,000 people, and processed between 600,000 and 700,000 hogs every year. To cure all that meat, Kingan & Co. annually used about 14 million pounds of salt.

From the beginning, Kingan & Co. was an innovative facility. Employees invented their own machinery, and the company found new ways to use slaughterhouse byproducts. Its most important invention, though, was a revolutionary refrigeration system that enabled the plant to operate year-round, not just in the freezing winter months. One of the employees, George W. Stockman, placed a network of air pipes into large vats containing ice and salt, and the air cooled to freezing as it flowed through the pipes.

"I inspected this plant one hot day in July," wrote historian Jacob Piatt Dunn, "and the room where the dressed hogs hung looked like a limestone cave with its coating of frost, and stalactites of white ice hanging from the rafters." Dunn suggested that "if Indianapolis wants to put up a monument to a citizen who did more for the world than all her professional men and statesmen put together, she has the subject in George W. Stockman."

So, selling sliced bacon was just another of many innovations for Kingan. At the time, customers bought hunks of bacon at the butcher shop and sliced them at home. Kingan's Reliable Bacon was sliced to a uniform thickness, which made it easier to cook. And, as one advertisement boasted in 1922, "You can use every ounce of it. No rind. No waste of any kind."

In 1952, Kingan & Co. was purchased by a Michigan company, which closed the facility in 1966.

Courtesy of the National Cancer Institute

Raggedy Ann and Raggedy Andy

Raggedy Ann's origin story—maybe true, maybe not—goes like this: One day, illustrator Johnny Gruelle was working in his home studio in Indianapolis when his daughter, Marcella, walked in. She was carrying a faceless rag doll she'd found in her grandmother's attic. Gruelle used one of his pens to draw a new face on the doll. Then he picked up a poetry book by James Whitcomb Riley, a family friend, and merged the titles of two poems—"The Raggedy Man" and "Little Orphant Annie"—to create the name Raggedy Ann.

Although he was born in Illinois, Gruelle grew up in the Lockerbie neighborhood of Indianapolis. As an adult, he became the first staff

illustrator for the *Indianapolis Star*, and he moved his young family to the Irvington neighborhood.

His wife, Myrtle, claimed that it was Gruelle himself, not their daughter, who found the doll. "There was something he wanted from the attic," she recalled. "While he was rummaging around for it, he found an old rag doll his mother had made for his sister. He said then that the doll would make a good story."

The timing of the attic discovery is unclear. But in the fall of 1915, Gruelle was granted a patent for "a new, original, and ornamental design for a doll." The first book featuring the character, *Raggedy Ann Stories*, made its debut in 1918. Raggedy Andy, with the same button eyes and red hair, joined the family in 1920. In all, Gruelle wrote more than 40 books about the two adventurous rag dolls.

"The Raggedys weren't ever simply dolls," wrote Gruelle biographer Patricia Hall. "They were literary characters, as well, possessing attributes and outlooks reflecting trustworthiness, kindness, and spunk."

Marcella, unfortunately, wasn't able to see her rag doll transformed into a national icon. She died in 1915, at the age of 13. According to family legend, Gruelle always kept the original Raggedy Ann in his studio as a reminder of his daughter.

The Vajen-Bader Smoke Protector

One of the oddest-looking inventions in Indianapolis history might also have been the most meaningful. In 1896, hardware salesman Willis C. Vajen patented the Vajen-Baden Smoke Protector, a helmet for firefighters. It enabled them to breathe fresh air in the midst of smoke and toxic gases. "Of the many useful articles that are manufactured in Indianapolis, there are none that have attracted greater attention than [this] product," stated *Hyman's Hand Book of Indianapolis* in 1897. By then, the $100 helmet was in use by firefighters in more than 100 of the largest cities worldwide, and the company had overseas agents in Johannesburg, London, and Yokohama.

The Vajen-Bader helmet was made of asbestos-tanned leather and held in place by two straps under the arms. Attached was a metal reservoir that could hold up to 100 pounds of compressed air, enough to last up to two hours. The helmet had ear pieces for hearing, mica-covered glass windows—with revolving cleaning brushes—for seeing, and a whistle for signaling.

"Light in weight, cheap, and durable, the helmet is scientifically perfect, and firemen by its use will be enabled to venture into the thickest smoke without fear of suffocation," read an 1895 article in the *Los Angeles Herald*.

In Indianapolis, firefighters first used the helmets in September 1896, after an ammonia explosion at Schmidt's Brewery, a subsidiary of the Indianapolis Brewing Company. The ammonia fumes were so strong that firemen couldn't get near the fire to extinguish it—until they put on their Vajen-Bader helmets.

Unsurprisingly, the helmet was a hit at firefighting conventions. During a convention in Salt Lake City in 1896, the *Salt Lake Herald* published a testimonial from George C. Hale, the fire chief in Kansas City, Missouri. Hale wrote that he and his men had dug a hole in a cellar, filling it with "the worst-smelling conglomerations of combustibles ever heaped together." When the smoke was too dense to see through, one of the men put on the helmet and went down into the cellar. He stayed there so long that his colleagues thought he might be unconscious, or worse. He emerged after 18 minutes. When asked how he could stand being down there so long, the fireman said, "Stand it? Why, I could have stayed down there all day."

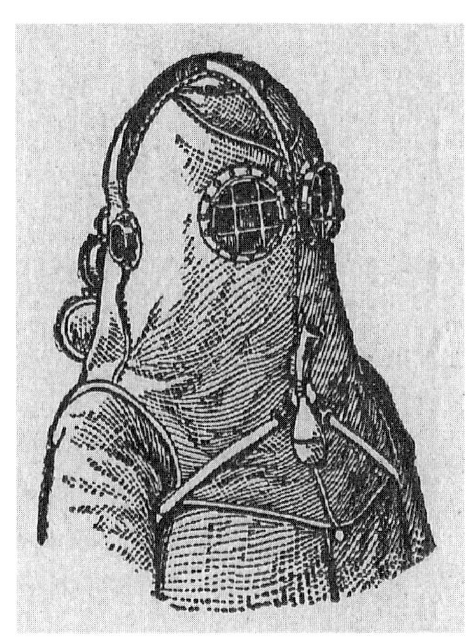

The First Machine Gun

During the Civil War, inventor Richard J. Gatling lived close to Union Depot. He watched as soldiers boarded trains for the battlefield, and he watched again as their bodies came home in boxes—often due to disease rather than battlefield injuries. "The thought then struck me, if a gun could be invented that would do the work of a hundred men, and would require but a few men to operate it, that the horrors of war would be greatly diminished, and an end would come much sooner of every struggle," he later told the *Indianapolis Journal*. "More men could stay home, and lives would be saved."

Previously, Gatling had focused on inventing farm equipment. But in November 1862 he secured a patent for his rapid-fire machine gun, which had six revolving barrels that could be turned and fired by a hand crank. Built in Indianapolis, the first model was capable of firing up to 250 bullets per minute.

One of Gatling's colleagues then demonstrated the weapon in Washington, and Indiana Gov. Oliver P. Morton gave his enthusiastic endorsement. But the head of the US Army Ordnance Department was unimpressed.

"[He] was an old fogy," Gatling said. "He believed flint-lock muskets were, on the whole, the best weapons for warfare."

One commanding officer, however, saw the merits of the guns, and he risked his career by buying them without permission. The guns were first used at the Battle of Petersburg, where "they created great consternation and slaughter, and the news of them went all over the world," Gatling said.

Soon the Gatling gun was in use by militaries worldwide. Gatling made continual improvements, and by 1884 the guns could fire up

Courtesy of the Library of Congress

to 1,200 bullets per minute. And Gatling still believed that the guns ultimately saved lives.

"Mr. Gatling, of Gatling gun fame, is a benevolent-looking old gentleman, with snowy hair and whiskers," the *Indianapolis Journal* reported. "He is slightly deaf, wears gold-rimmed spectacles, and talks about his wholesale slaughtering machine as unconcernedly as though it were merely an improved hay-rake."

Ray Harroun in the winning Marmon Wasp. Courtesy of IMS Photo

The Rearview Mirror

Since 1909, the Indianapolis Motor Speedway has been a testing ground for new innovations in automobiles, such as front-wheel drive, more durable tires, and even seatbelts. The most famous, however, is the rearview mirror, which was invented for the first Indianapolis 500 in 1911.

Seven years earlier, future racecar driver Ray Harroun had worked as a chauffeur in Chicago. While sitting in traffic one day, he noticed something odd: a horse-drawn taxicab with a mirror attached to a pole, enabling the driver to see the traffic behind him. *That's a good idea*, Harroun must have thought, and he made a mental note.

In the early years of auto racing, racecars were designed to carry two people: the driver and a mechanic. The mechanic not only maintained the vehicle during the race but also warned the driver about the traffic coming up behind him. In 1911, as Harroun—now a racecar driver—strategized about how to win the first Indianapolis 500, he decided to make his car lighter by leaving the mechanic in the pit. His competitors objected for safety reasons. How could he avoid collisions if he didn't know about the cars behind him? Harroun remembered that horse-drawn taxicab, and he answered their objections by fitting his car with the first rearview mirror.

Harroun went on to win that first race in his Marmon Wasp, but not because of the rearview mirror. He calculated that if he limited his speed to about 75 miles per hour, his tires would last much longer, and he would reduce the number of time-consuming pitstops. Instead of pushing his car to its limits, he won the race by making smart choices. The Wasp is now on display—alongside many other winning cars—at the Indianapolis Motor Speedway Museum.

A Record-Setting Sports Venue

With more than 250,000 seats, the Indianapolis Motor Speedway is the largest sports venue in the world. Because of this, the Indianapolis 500—the "greatest spectacle in racing"—is the world's largest single-day spectator sporting event.

The Transistor Radio

You are, at this moment, surrounded by transistors, which regulate the flow of electricity in circuits. In your phone and smart watch, in your TV and remote control, in your laptop, in your appliances, and in your car—they are everywhere. And it all got started here in Indianapolis, where a local company manufactured the first consumer product that contained transistors.

The product was the Regency TR-1, a portable radio. It wasn't the first portable radio. But it was the first to replace inefficient vacuum tubes with transistors, giving the product a huge boost in battery life: 20 to 30 hours, compared with just three to five hours for older models.

In 1953, Texas Instruments—now best known for its calculators—started manufacturing transistors under a license from Bell Labs. The company wanted to use the transistors in a small radio, but at the time it had no experience with consumer products.

Courtesy of Joe Haupt, Wikimedia Commons

So, Texas Instruments partnered with Indianapolis-based Industrial Development Engineering Associates (IDEA), which manufactured TV signal boosters. Working on a very tight timeframe, engineers at IDEA further refined the circuit, miniaturized the other radio parts, and started manufacturing the TR-1 (under the brand name Regency) in time for an October 1954 release. The product weighed only 11 ounces and cost $49.95, the equivalent of about $600 today.

IDEA projected sales of 20 million radios within three years, but in the first year only about 100,000 units were sold. *Consumer Reports* gave the radio a poor review because of its sound quality and urged readers to "await further developments before buying." It also seems that Texas Instruments and IDEA misread the market. It was the height of the Cold War, and they expected American families to buy Regency TR-1s for their bomb shelters and emergency kits. They missed the fact that teenagers listening to the new rock and roll music might want radios of their own.

However, "Texas Instruments did earn a huge dividend from the Regency TR-1, for this shirt-pocket portable demonstrated to all in the know that the transistor age had arrived," wrote Michael Brian Schiffer in *The Portable Radio in American Life*. As a result, IBM switched from vacuum tubes to transistors in its computers. And when IBM engineers complained that it couldn't be done, the company president—who had purchased hundreds of TR-1s—would hand over one of the radios and walk away.

Eli Lilly's Insulin Breakthrough

Before the 1920s, diabetes was a death sentence. A child diagnosed with the disease could expect to live less than a year, and the only treatment was a starvation-level diet to slow the progress of the illness. But in 1921, researchers from the University of Toronto developed insulin. They then partnered with Eli Lilly & Co., which pioneered the manufacturing process for the life-saving medication.

For the researchers, partnering with Lilly required a leap of faith. The company was "one of the most important concerns in this city and one of the largest of its class in the country," declared *Hyman's Hand Book of Indianapolis.* Yet Lilly had launched its biochemical research department only a few years earlier, in 1919, and it still manufactured traditional patent medicines. Its best-selling product was Succus Alterans, aka "Alternative Juice," an all-purpose elixir for skin and blood diseases.

That changed in October 1923, when Lilly began shipping the world's first commercial insulin, sold under the brand name Iletin. By 1925, the company was distributing more than 200 million units of insulin per year. "Newspaper stories

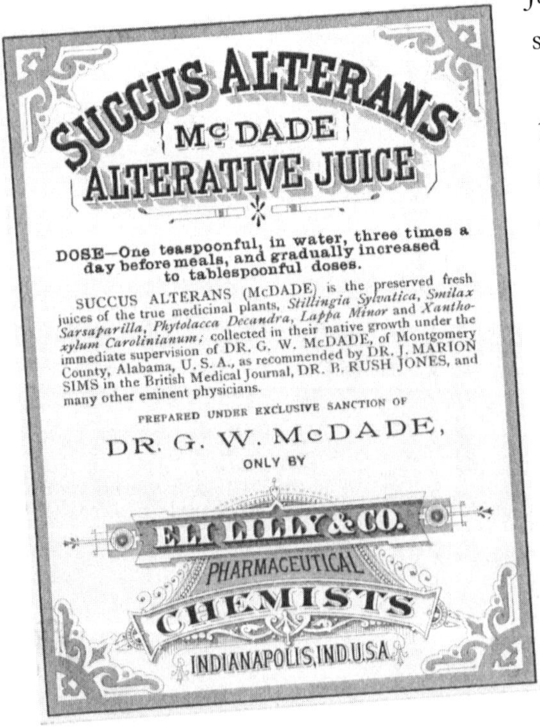

Courtesy of the Library of Congress

told of diabetics revived from their deathbeds by the wonder drug," wrote one Lilly biographer. The medication positioned Lilly as an international leader in research-based pharmaceutical manufacturing.

The wonder drug was also a boon for Indianapolis. In 1937, the Lilly family founded the Lilly Endowment with a large gift of company stock. Since then, the endowment has distributed nearly $14 billion in grants to more than 10,000 arts and community organizations, many of them based in Indianapolis.

A Deadly Cure

Another medical breakthrough came from the pathology department at Central State Hospital, a psychiatric facility. In the 1930s, 30 percent of admissions were due to syphilis, which can cause dementia. A decade earlier, an Austrian psychiatrist had discovered that syphilis could be cured by malaria. Central State won international recognition for improving the malarial therapy technique and for experimenting with different strains of the disease. The downside was that patients occasionally died of malaria.

"Abe Martin" creator Kin Hubbard. Courtesy of Bass Photo Co. Collection, Indiana Historical Society

Chapter Two

Overlooked Locals

Later on in this book, we'll talk about the famous people who call Indianapolis home. But this chapter is about the Hoosiers you haven't heard of yet. They include a best-selling writer who has faded from our collective memory, as well as one of the most successful composers of ragtime music. The list also includes a prolific painter, a chart-topping musical group, and a humorist whose work once appeared in newspapers across the country.

This chapter also highlights local heroes, including several police officers who deserve a moment in the spotlight. You'll also read about Walter Bedell Smith, who negotiated the surrender of Nazi Germany. And we can't forget Madge Oberholtzer, the woman who—at great personal cost—single-handedly brought down the KKK in Central Indiana. As Kurt Vonnegut once said, "I don't know what it is about Hoosiers. But wherever you go, there is always a Hoosier doing something very important there."

The Ragtime Composer: May Frances Aufderheide

The syncopated rhythms of ragtime are synonymous with composer Scott Joplin, but Indianapolis has its own ragtime claim to fame in May Frances Aufderheide. Although her career was short, she was one of the nation's most successful composers—male or female—of ragtime tunes for the piano.

Aufderheide was born into an upper-middle-class family in 1888, the same year the Statehouse and Union Station were completed. As a child, she studied piano with her aunt, who performed with the Indianapolis Symphony. But classical music wasn't her style; she wanted to play music that was exciting and new.

After attending finishing school and taking a grand tour of Europe with her parents, Aufderheide married in March 1908. The newlyweds moved to Richmond, Indiana, and in the early years of her marriage, her creativity flourished. That same year Aufderheide published her first composition, "Dusty Rag," which sold well enough that her father opened a music publishing business as a sideline. Although the business has been "criticized

Courtesy of the Library of Congress

as a vanity press for his daughter's compositions," it became an important publisher of Indiana ragtime composers.

Between 1908 and 1912, Aufderheide published 19 ragtime compositions, seven of which were commercially successful. They included "Thriller Rag," "Richmond Rag," "Buzzer Rag," "A Totally Different Rag," and "Blue Ribbon Rag." In August 1909, the *American Music and Art Journal* reported that Aufderheide's compositions were in considerable demand because they were "delightfully and persistently infectious."

In 1913, she and her husband moved back to Indianapolis. For unknown reasons, Aufderheide stopped composing, possibly because ragtime was losing ground to jazz. The couple moved to California in 1947, and Aufderheide died there in 1972.

The "Other" National Anthem

Baseball fans can thank Indianapolis for the beloved tune "Take Me Out to the Ball Game." The music was written by Indy native Albert Von Tilzer, with lyrics by Jack Norworth. The latter was inspired by a baseball advertisement on a subway train. The song was a hit in 1908, and in 2008 it received the Towering Song Award from the Songwriters Hall of Fame as one of the most recognizable tunes in the nation. The song, sometimes called America's "other" national anthem, has also been honored on a US postage stamp.

Courtesy of Tage Olsin, Wikimedia Commons

The Writer: Meredith Nicholson

Courtesy of the Indiana Historical Society

In the early 1900s, Indiana was known for its "Big Four" authors: James Whitcomb Riley, Booth Tarkington, George Ade, and Meredith Nicholson. The names of Riley and Tarkington are still recognized today, at least locally. Ade wasn't from Indianapolis, so we can ignore him. But Nicholson—who wrote some of the best-selling novels of the era—deserves more attention than he receives.

Born in Crawfordsville in 1866 and raised in Indianapolis, Nicholson abandoned his formal education during his freshman year in high school. But he was a voracious reader with wide-ranging interests, and he educated himself well. At age 20 he became a newspaper reporter. He also began to publish poetry on the side, but "his talents clearly lay elsewhere," a biographer remarked.

In 1900 Nicholson published *The Hoosiers*, a book of essays about the state's literary history. The book was well received and gave him the confidence to become a full-time writer. In 1903 he published his first novel, *The Main Chance*, which sold well. And in 1905 he published his most famous novel, *The House of a Thousand Candles*, which was a runaway best-seller. The "swashbuckling, thrilling adventure" was set in Indiana; he called it "a fairy tale with pistols." Later in his career, Nicholson moved away from romantic thrillers toward more realistic literature. The best example is 1913's *The Hoosier Chronicle*, which he set in Indianapolis. In all, Nicholson wrote nearly 30 books.

The Great Depression put Nicholson in a financial bind, and he was relieved in 1933 to be offered the post of US ambassador to Paraguay. Later he served as a diplomat in both Venezuela and Nicaragua. Despite his wanderings, he remained a proud Hoosier throughout his life. He once joked, "It is inconceivable that anyone fully advised as to Indiana's greatness would live elsewhere unless forcibly restrained by legal process."

Another Big Four

Indianapolis writer Booth Tarkington is one of only four people in history to twice win the Pulitzer Prize for fiction—for *The Magnificent Ambersons and Alice Adams*. The other three are William Faulkner, John Updike, and Colson Whitehead.

Courtesy of the Library of Congress

The Humorist: Kin Hubbard

Though he gets little recognition today, Frank McKinney "Kin" Hubbard was perhaps the nation's most influential Hoosier in the early 1900s. In 1904 he created the folksy Abe Martin cartoon for the *Indianapolis News*, and eventually the character was syndicated in more than 300 newspapers across the country. "The homely philosophy, pointed wit, and aptness of Abe's sayings spread from coast to coast, and were quoted everywhere," read his obituary in the *Indianapolis Star*.

Born in Ohio in 1868, Hubbard left school before seventh grade. At the time, his life ambition was to become "the sole proprietor of a good, well-painted, comprehensive one-ring circus." He worked odd jobs until his sketches attracted the attention of John H. Holliday, the publisher of the *News*, who hired him as a political cartoonist. After three years, Hubbard was fired by a new managing editor, but the *News* hired him back in 1901. Three years later, Abe Martin was born, and the fictional resident of Brown County appeared on the back page of the *News* daily for 26 years—always with a witty, common-sense observation expressed in a backwoods accent. In 1910, Hoosier author George Ade wrote about the Abe Martin character for a national magazine, and the syndication offers rolled in.

Hubbard died of a heart attack on December 26, 1930. Author Meredith Nicholson wrote at the time, "We have had in Indiana no clearer case of genius than that presented by Kin Hubbard." And humorist Will Rogers told a reporter, "Kin Hubbard was at the top for real downright humor." Since Hubbard's death, some Abe Martin sayings have aged poorly, but others still feel insightful and relevant.

The Wisdom of Abe Martin

Selected quotes from Kin Hubbard's Abe Martin character:

- **"It's no disgrace t' be poor, but it might as well be."**
- **"What comes easy goes easy—unless it's relatives."**
- **"Boys will be boys, an' so will lots o' ole men."**
- **"Ther' never kin be any real happiness where ther's bad coffee."**
- **"You never know a feller till you go fishin' with him."**
- **"So live that you won't be afraid t' run fer mayor."**

The Fighter: Madge Oberholtzer

In the 1920s, D. C. Stephenson claimed to be above the law. He was a Grand Dragon of the Ku Klux Klan at a time when up to 40 percent of native-born white men in Indianapolis were dues-paying members. Stephenson decided who would win elections, and in return politicians pledged their loyalty to him.

Courtesy of the Indiana State Library

One night at a political dinner, he met fellow Irvington resident Madge Oberholtzer. A career woman in her late 20s, she managed a program that provided books to children in rural areas. She and Stephenson met socially a few times afterward, but that was the extent of their connection.

Then, on March 15, 1925, Madge returned home from a date around 10 p.m. to learn that Stephenson had been calling all day. She called him back, and he demanded that she come to his home immediately to discuss "urgent business." She reluctantly agreed, forgetting her hat in her haste. When she arrived, she found Stephenson drunk and armed. Surrounded by his bodyguards, she was dragged to Union Station, where she was forced into a private sleeper car on a train bound for Chicago. Stephenson then raped and assaulted her, leaving her covered in bruises and bite marks.

The following morning, Madge was given some money to buy a hat. Although escorted by a bodyguard, she also managed to buy bichloride of mercury, a household disinfectant. She took six tablets, thinking it was her only way out. She repeatedly begged for medical care, but Stephenson said she could see a doctor only if she married him, so that she could not testify against him in court. She refused.

Desperately ill, she was eventually taken home. There, she made a dying declaration so frank and detailed that it is still used as an example in law school textbooks. It is often said that Madge died by suicide, but the actual cause of her death on April 14 was sepsis. One of her wounds had become badly infected.

The public's sympathy was strongly with Madge, and Stephenson was convicted of murder. He expected a pardon from the governor, and when he didn't receive one, he retaliated by releasing evidence of bribery and corruption at every level of city and state government. KKK membership plummeted, and the Klan lost its hold on Indiana politics—all because Madge was brave enough to speak the truth.

The Police Officer: William Whitfield

When police officer William Whitfield died on November 24, 1922, his death merited only a single small paragraph in the *Indianapolis Times.* Although he had been shot in the line of duty, there was no official police funeral, and flags were not flown at half-mast. No detective was ever assigned to investigate his murder, which remains unsolved. All of this because Whitfield was Black.

Whitfield had been patrolling the area near College Avenue and 36th Street when he stopped a man to question him. The man started to run away, then turned and fired one shot into Whitfield's abdomen. Despite the injury, Whitfield tried to chase the suspect, and the two exchanged gunfire. Whitfield was then taken by car to one of the only local hospitals that treated Black patients.

A small article in the next day's *Indianapolis Star* was titled, "Negro Cop Shot by White Man." It mentioned that Whitfield, age 37, had joined the force in 1910 and "has an exceptionally good record." The next day, the newspaper announced that police were seeking a potential witness. After that, the *Star* was

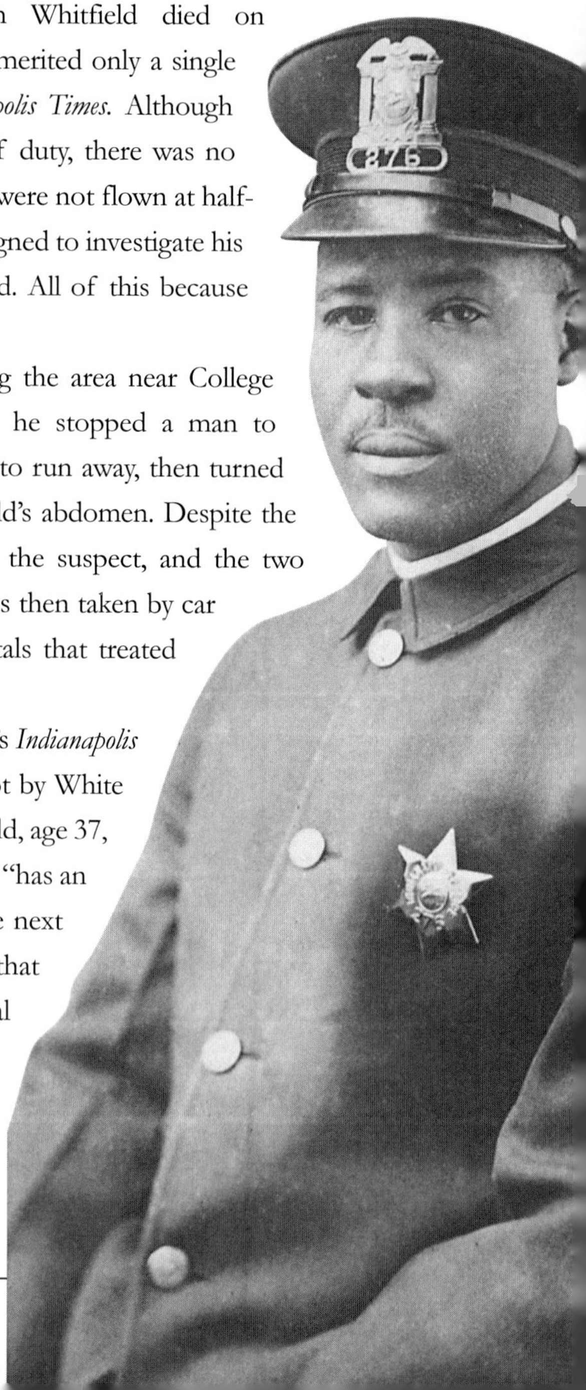

William Whitfield
Courtesy of Indianapolis Metropolitan Police Department

silent on the issue, and the case was forgotten. For 75 years, Whitfield lay in an unmarked grave at Crown Hill Cemetery.

Thankfully, the case didn't stay forgotten. In 1998, an article about Whitfield appeared in the police department newsletter. Within three hours, enough money had been raised to pay for a gravestone. That November, more than 200 people attended a long-overdue memorial service for Whitfield, with honor guard ceremonies and a 21-gun salute. The stone reads: "Patrolman William Whitfield, 1885–1922. First black officer to make the supreme sacrifice in the line of duty."

The Death of Hugh Burns

The first Indianapolis police officer to die in the line of duty was Hugh Burns in 1883. Although he was off duty and not in uniform, an employee at a local boardinghouse knew him and asked him to help break up a fight. He was shot as soon as he came through the door. The shooter, John Jeter, successfully claimed self-defense because he had not known that Burns was a police officer.

Hugh Burns
Courtesy of Indianapolis Metropolitan Police Department

The Police Officer: Emma Christy Baker

In 1918, the Indianapolis Metropolitan Police Department launched a bold experiment. With so many men off fighting in WWI, perhaps women could fill the department's vacancies? On June 15 the department swore in 13 female police officers, two of whom were Black, and one female police sergeant, Clara Burnside.

Emma Christy Baker was part of this group, and she became the first female IMPD officer to work outside of a police station. A graduate of Shortridge High School, Baker was well-known in the community because her father owned a successful laundry business. She was assigned to patrol in plainclothes downtown, primarily on Indiana Avenue, and to investigate gambling, prostitution, petty theft, and the like.

Emma Christy Baker
Courtesy of Indianapolis Metropolitan Police Department

It was an unlikely opportunity for Baker. Her mother had been enslaved until the age of 5, and her parents had come to Indianapolis to escape racial harassment in more rural Salem, Indiana. Baker was born in 1865, only two years after President Abraham Lincoln signed the Emancipation Proclamation.

In 1922, Baker was transferred to the probation division's juvenile court. One of her jobs was to patrol dance halls, which were off limits to underage youth. By 1927 the department had 22 female officers, making it the largest such unit in the world. That year 17 of them—Baker included—were dismissed, but the women were soon reinstated because the department hadn't followed the proper termination procedures. The unit was disbanded again in the 1930s, this time permanently, but Baker stayed on the force as a jail matron until her retirement in 1939.

Baker died in 1955 and was buried in Crown Hill Cemetery without a headstone—an injustice that was rectified in 2003.

A Pioneering Firefighter

Indianapolis's first female firefighter was Bryona Slaughter, who joined the department to great fanfare in 1978. A self-identified tomboy, Slaughter had previously worked as a short-order cook, and being a firefighter "was just a job opportunity that came up," she told the *Indianapolis Star*, which also asked how doing such difficult work would affect her "feminine image" and her family schedule. Slaughter's time with the department was short and tumultuous: she was fired in October 1978, was reinstated in May 1979, and resigned that August.

The Soldier: Walter Bedell Smith

The man who negotiated the surrender of Nazi Germany in 1945 was neither the US president nor General Dwight D. Eisenhower, the commander of the Allied European forces. Rather, it was Indianapolis native Walter Bedell Smith, who at the time was Eisenhower's chief of staff. He informed the Germans that "there was nothing to discuss except the immediate surrender of all German forces," and he himself signed the official documents that ended the war in Europe.

A graduate of Manual High School, Smith started his military career with the Indiana National Guard. By the time of the Nazi surrender he had risen to the rank of brigadier general in the US Army, and a few years later he was promoted to general.

Smith's service to his country did not end with the war. From 1946 to 1948, he served as the US ambassador to the Soviet Union, just as the Cold War was heating up. Then, in 1950, he reluctantly accepted a dinky little post that no one else wanted: he became the director of the Central Intelligence Agency.

"Before Smith became [director], CIA was regarded in Washington as an upstart organization of no real consequence, and many Americans had not even heard of the agency," wrote a CIA historian. By the time Smith left the agency, however, it "had assumed a preeminent status in the intelligence community."

Smith was "an exacting, hard-hitting executive who brooked neither mediocrity nor ineptitude." He reorganized the CIA into the directorate system that still defines its structure today. He initiated the practice of delivering a daily intelligence briefing to the president, and he solidified the country's intelligence relationship with the United Kingdom. He also

Courtesy of Harris & Ewing, Harry S. Truman Library

created the position of inspector general to increase accountability. He "arguably was CIA's most successful and influential director because of the legacy he left," the historian wrote.

His next post was undersecretary of the State Department. Even after he retired in 1954, he continued to serve on advisory panels related to defense and national security. He died in 1961, and he is buried at Arlington National Cemetery.

The Artist: Felrath Hines

For decades, Indianapolis native Felrath Hines managed two parallel careers. He was an expert in art restoration and conservation, and eventually he became chief conservator at the National Portrait Gallery—the first Black person to hold that post. But he was also an artist in his own right, known for his "distinctive contributions to modernist abstract painting."

Born in 1913, Hines grew up in an 800-square-foot house on West 25th Street. He was among the first students to attend the segregated Crispus Attucks High School. As a teenager, he won scholarships to attend Saturday drawing and painting classes at the John Herron Art Institute. "I had this feeling I could do something with a paint brush, and it was like a revelation," he later said.

Courtesy of The N. Jay Jaffee Trust

Hines's path to art conservation was a winding one. He joined the Civilian Conservation Corps after high school, then moved north to attend the Art Institute of Chicago. He took classes by day and worked as a dining-car waiter for the Chicago & North Western Railroad by night. Then, in

1946, he moved to New York City, where he continued to take classes but also apprenticed himself to a fine art framer. He met many artists and art conservators in that role, and in the late 1950s he left the framing business, apprenticing himself to several prominent conservators. He also co-founded Spiral, a group of Black artists who were active in the civil rights movement. Meanwhile his paintings became more and more abstract.

As a conservator, one of Hines's clients was Georgia O'Keeffe, and she was the one who recommended him for the position of chief conservator at the National Portrait Gallery. He retired from conservation in the mid-1980s, and then he began to paint more prolifically than ever. He died in 1993. His works are now in the collections of the Smithsonian American Art Museum, the Museum of Fine Arts Boston, the Indianapolis Museum of Art at Newfields, and the National Museum of African American History and Culture, among many others.

The Crooners: The Ink Spots

The Circle City was the starting point for the Ink Spots, prolific hit-makers who became the first Black performers to appear on the *Ed Sullivan Show.* Inspired by vaudeville and jazz, the group laid the template for doo-wop and modern R&B with "a tradition of romantic, bluesy ballads sung in perfect harmony."

The original members, Orville "Hoppy" Jones, Ivory "Deek" Watson, Charlie Fuqua, and Jerry Daniels, started performing here in the late 1920s. In the early 1930s, the group relocated to New York City, where they performed at Harlem's legendary Apollo Theatre in 1934. The following year they were signed by RCA Victor Records, which organized a European tour, but none of the early recordings hit the charts. Dropped by their first label, the band later signed with Decca Records and replaced Daniels with Bill Kenny, who was to become the star.

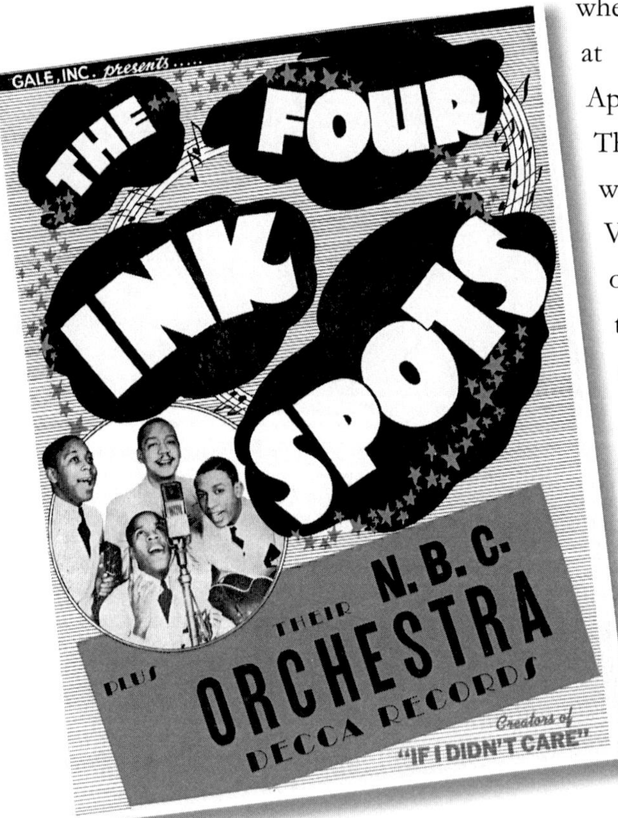

Courtesy of the Smithsonian

Kenny introduced the Ink Spots to a new singing style called "top to bottom." His high tenor would carry the melody through the first part of a song, then Jones would speak the words in his low bass voice. The group's breakthrough song in this style was 1939's "If I Didn't Care," which is still one of the best-selling singles of all time, just ahead of Celine Dion's "My Heart Will Go On" and Mariah Carey's "All I Want for Christmas Is You."

The Ink Spots went on to have 30 hit songs in the 1940s, among them a collaboration with Ella Fitzgerald. They also appeared as musical groups in the films *The Great American Broadcast* and Abbott and Costello's *Pardon My Sarong*. And they broke down racial barriers by headlining concerts in previously segregated Southern venues, such as the Carlo Club in Miami in 1948.

Unfortunately, the band's membership was always unstable, with 20 people performing as part of the group over the years. The group dealt with illness, infighting, and even legal battles, and it finally dissolved in 1954. Although they are little known in Indianapolis today, the Ink Spots were inducted into the Grammy Hall of Fame in 1987 and the Rock and Roll Hall of Fame in 1989.

Top of the Charts

The greatest hits for the Ink Spots included "If I Didn't Care," "Address Unknown," "My Prayer," "We Three (My Echo, My Shadow, and Me)," "I Don't Want to Set the World on Fire," and "Into Each Life Some Rain Must Fall."

Courtesy of the Indiana
Historical Society

WANTED

IN 5 STATES

JOHN DILLINGER

PUBLIC ENEMY NUMBER ONE!

The Attorney General of the U.S. has authorized a

$20,000 REWARD!

for information leading to the arrest of John Dillinger.

Chapter Three

The Criminal Element

These are the darker tales of Indianapolis, including legendary murders both solved and unsolved. This chapter also includes a hostage crisis that became a media circus, a bomb that injured a small child, and a massive grave-robbing conspiracy that left some Indianapolis cemeteries practically empty. John Dillinger gets a mention, of course, as does our homegrown (alleged) serial killer, Herb Baumeister.

Fortunately, some of these stories have a humorous side. Examples include a police mutiny supported by the mayor himself, as well as a Civil War "battle" that wasn't a battle at all. Here you'll also find tales of the city's first jailbreak, the humiliating defeat of its worst bully, and the downfall of two respected pharmacists. There's also—yes, really—the tale of the volunteer firefighters who became prolific arsonists. Whether serious or ridiculous, these crimes all shaped the Indianapolis of today.

The Christmas Jailbreak

On Christmas Day in 1821, the fledgling Indianapolis had unwanted visitors. A group of four Kentucky boatmen arrived on a keelboat in the wee hours, looking for holiday fun. The men, already drunk, were disappointed to find that Daniel Larkins's grocery store was closed. But if liquor couldn't be bought, the men were willing to steal it instead, and they attempted to break into the store. (Another version of the story says the men got drunk at the store and then started to smash it up.) Either way, one historian described it as "the first especially exciting incident in the quiet course of the settlement."

Locals heard the commotion, and soon a crowd had gathered. The Kentuckians were asked to stop, but "they responded with a defiance backed by knives." Early settler James Blake offered to tackle the leader of the group if the rest of the crowd could handle the other men, and this was done. The town then held an impromptu trial at the home of Squire McIlvain, a justice of the peace.

The problem was that McIlvain's powers were limited. He could fine each man a maximum of $3, but more serious crimes had to be referred to the circuit court. Even worse, the nearest jail was in Connersville. Nobody wanted to trek 60 miles through the forest late at night, in the dead of winter, to escort the four men to jail—especially on Christmas Day. A different solution was needed.

First, the settlers made a big show of forming a posse to haul the Kentuckians to jail the next morning. Then they imprisoned the men overnight in an empty log cabin. The guards, however, were instructed to be less than vigilant. Sometime during the night, the four prisoners escaped from the cabin and vanished, never to be seen in Indianapolis again. This, of course, had been the plan all along.

A Daring Escape

The Marion County Jail experienced its own jailbreak on July 4, 1920. Twenty-four federal inmates sawed through their bars and escaped, and the jailer—who was asleep—didn't notice for almost an hour. He was alerted only when the police arrested two of the escapees in connection with a mugging. Most of the men were rounded up quickly, but safecracker Arthur Welling remained at large for a year and a half.

Burkhart and the Chain Gang

In the 1830s, Indianapolis's most notorious troublemaker was a man named David Burkhart. He was "a square-built, red-headed, muscular fellow, who prided himself on his fighting abilities," and he was the leader of a "lawless crowd" that called itself the Chain Gang. When not employed in manual labor, gang members stole local farmers' chickens, destroyed their fences, and harassed the city's Black residents. The group "kept the northwestern corner of the town in a perpetual turmoil," one historian wrote. But 1836 was a turning point for the group.

In March of that year, the Chain Gang attacked the wrong person, a well-connected Black businessman named James Overall. He defended his home with a shotgun, injuring a member of the gang, and the group fled. But they shouted death threats along the way, and Overall took them seriously. He sought the help of attorney Calvin Fletcher, who rounded up a group of law-abiding citizens to protect Overall. One member of the Chain Gang, David Leach, was arrested, and Burkhart briefly left town.

Perhaps still smarting from that defeat, Burkhart turned up again one evening at an outdoor worship service. He appeared at the edge of the crowd, drunk, dirty, and barefoot, loudly singing a lewd song. The preacher called for silence, but Burkhart kept singing. Legend says the preacher then descended from the pulpit and punched Burkhart in the face, knocking him unconscious.

Whether or not that legend is true, Burkhart was charged with disturbing the peace, and in court the next day he was defiant. Attorney Samuel Merrill decided to beat Burkhart at his own game; he challenged him to a wrestling match. "The rowdy was heavily and easily thrown by the sober and muscular lawyer, greatly to his chagrin and the discomfiture of the gang," said one account of the incident.

Samuel Merrill
Courtesy of the Indiana Historical Society

Unsurprisingly, Burkhart left town soon afterward, this time permanently. Not much is known about his later life, although he appears to have settled down. Several other members of the Chain Gang, however, met with violent deaths.

A Legal Challenge

At the time when David Leach was arrested for threatening James Overall, Indiana law stated that a Black person could not testify against a white person in court. Leach argued that his arrest was unlawful because it was based on Overall's testimony, but a judge ruled that Overall had the right to "avail himself of the remedies prescribed by law."

Courtesy of Bass Photo Co. Collection, Indiana Historical Society

The Antics of the Volunteer Firefighters

Here is true irony: some of the most prolific arsonists in Indianapolis history were its volunteer firefighters.

In the Circle City's earliest years, settlers fought fires themselves, and a town ordinance required every household to own a fire bucket. After the first Statehouse was built, the city and state split the cost of a hand-pumped fire engine, and in 1837 the first firehouse was built on the north side of Monument Circle. It was staffed by the new Marion Fire

Company. The firemen were unpaid volunteers, but they were exempt from jury duty and local taxes. Membership thrived, and new volunteer companies popped up all over the city.

It soon became difficult to control the rowdy groups. They broke into "houses of ill repute" and flooded the buildings, they caused political havoc, and they competed fiercely to get "first water" on local fires. When an insurance company announced a prize in 1849 for the company that got first water on the most fires that year, the city's vacant buildings one by one went up in smoke.

Then members of the Marion Fire Company began to complain about poor living conditions in their firehouse. When they were denied funding for a new building, the firehouse mysteriously burned to the ground. Some city records were destroyed, but all of the firefighters' possessions were miraculously saved.

By 1859 the city council had had enough, and it approved funding for a paid fire department. The volunteer firefighters were furious, and for months many companies refused to return the city's firefighting equipment. That November, 31 paid firemen officially replaced more than 600 highly suspect volunteers.

Double Murder Leads to Media Frenzy

On the afternoon of September 12, 1868, Jacob and Nancy Jane Young went for a ride in their buggy. The next day they were found dead along a riverbank, in what came to be called the Cold Spring murders. Jacob had been shot with a rifle, and Nancy Jane had been shot with a pistol, then bludgeoned. Her body was partially burned, perhaps because a spark from the gun had ignited her crinoline.

The rifle was still lying next to Jacob Young, and the chief of police recognized it immediately. He had considered purchasing it for his own son, and the gun was easily traced to a Bill Abrams. Investigators soon learned that Abrams and Jacob Young, along with a woman named Nancy Clem, had been involved in a mysterious money racket, likely a Ponzi scheme that was starting to fall apart. Abrams and Clem were quickly arrested, as was Clem's brother, Silas Hartman.

The prosecutor's theory was that Abrams had purchased the gun and given it to Hartman. Clem had then gone on the buggy ride with the Youngs, with Hartman following at a distance. On the riverbank, Hartman had killed Jacob, and Clem had killed Nancy Jane. Then Hartman and Clem had robbed the couple of more than $7,000 in cash, which provided a motive.

The event was Indianapolis's first premeditated murder, and it became the city's first sensationalized media frenzy. Abrams was convicted of murder and sentenced to life in prison, although he received a pardon from the governor a decade later. Hartman died by suicide. Clem, however, was tried for the murders four times: a hung jury, a conviction that was overturned, a hung jury, and another conviction that was overturned. At that point, prosecutors gave up and set her free.

Courtesy of the Indiana Historical Society

Amazingly, Clem again started up her financial scheming. She was successfully sued by several people from whom she had borrowed money, and she was ultimately convicted of perjury in one of those lawsuits. She was sentenced to four years in prison, and the general feeling in town was that it was much less than she deserved.

Toward the end of her life, Clem became a successful salesperson for a patent medicine called Slavin's Infallible Female Tonic. Nearly 30 years after the murder she died of kidney inflammation, having maintained her innocence until the end.

The Grave-Robbing Conspiracy

In the fall of 1902, several Indianapolis residents received anonymous tips: their relatives' graves had been dug up, and the bodies could be found at the Central College of Physicians and Surgeons. The subsequent investigation led police to a syndicate of grave robbers led by a man named Rufus Cantrell, the "King of the Ghouls."

In the early 1900s, medical schools were moving away from lecture-based anatomy lessons to a more interactive teaching method—dissection. But without modern embalming techniques, the schools constantly needed new bodies. Legal channels couldn't meet the demand, creating a black market for fresh cadavers.

Cantrell cooperated with investigators from the start, admitting that he had robbed at least 100 graves in the past three months alone. Of Mount Jackson Cemetery, he said, "We pretty near cleaned the place out." He named seven of his fellow "resurrectionists." He also accused Dr. Joseph Alexander, a physician at Central College. Alexander routinely paid for bodies—usually $5 or $10—without asking questions. Not only that, he visited the State Board of Health each day to review death notices and identify fresh graves, information that he shared with Cantrell. Alexander was essentially placing orders.

A grand jury empaneled in mid-October returned 25 indictments against the ghouls (who were Black) and against five white Indianapolis physicians, including Alexander. His trial came first, and his defense team focused on destroying the credibility of Cantrell as a witness. The attorneys brought up Cantrell's criminal record and his discharge from the US Army due to epilepsy, which at the time was considered a mental illness. Alexander's attorneys also discredited Cantrell based on his race.

"King of the Ghouls" Rufus Cantrell
Courtesy of Indiana State Archives

In a closing statement, one attorney said, "Would you send a reputable citizen, well known for probity and honesty, to the penitentiary on lying statements of a Black, heinous, slimy creature like Cantrell?" He also called the grave robbers a "pack of beasts."

You can guess what happened. Alexander's trial ended in a hung jury, and he never paid for his crimes. Charges against the other physicians were dropped or simply never prosecuted. Meanwhile, Cantrell and his fellow ghouls went to prison.

The Murder of Dr. Knabe

Dr. Helene Knabe was a trailblazer for women in medicine—a strong, determined woman who shattered glass ceilings everywhere she went. But, like so many other women both then and now, she was murdered by her boyfriend (probably).

Born in Germany, Dr. Knabe came to Indianapolis in 1896. She knew what she wanted—to be a doctor—and thought the United States would provide her with better opportunities. She was a star pupil at the Medical College of Indiana, and she was teaching classes in pathology even before she graduated.

Courtesy of the Library of Congress

In 1905, Dr. Knabe took a job as assistant pathologist for the Indiana State Laboratory of Hygiene, where she investigated outbreaks of typhoid fever, diphtheria, and the like. She also became a recognized expert in rabies diagnosis. Two years later, she was promoted to superintendent of the lab. But she was promised a raise that never materialized, and she resigned after a year in that role. "They expect an employee in the lab to have a man's brain but be paid a woman's salary," she said at the time.

Starting in 1909, Dr. Knabe taught classes in parasitology at the Indiana Veterinary College, making her the first woman in the nation to hold such a position. She also ran her own medical practice; illustrated medical texts on the side; and taught community classes on first aid, hygiene, and safe food preservation. And, in the meantime, she developed a romantic relationship with a colleague, Dr. William B. Craig, and they planned to marry . . . until he changed his mind.

On the morning of October 24, 1911, Dr. Knabe's assistant found her dead in her bedroom, with her throat sliced open. Although the coroner ruled her death a murder, the superintendent of police made sexist assumptions and decided she had died by suicide—despite overwhelming evidence to the contrary. For two years, the police were guided by that false assumption. Finally, in 1913, Dr. Craig was indicted for her murder. The prosecution had plenty of evidence, but it was all circumstantial, and ultimately Dr. Craig was acquitted. Looking back at the case now, it seems likely that he got away with murder.

The 1913 Police Mutiny

"Protect the strikebreakers." That was the order Indianapolis police officers received during a labor strike in 1913. The employees of the Indianapolis Street Railway Company, which operated the city's streetcars, were on strike, and the company had imported hundreds of strikebreakers from Chicago. The strike turned into a days-long riot, in which many streetcars were vandalized and burned. At that point, the company refused to run the streetcar service unless the strikebreakers had police protection on each streetcar.

In all, 33 police officers mutinied, flatly refusing to protect the strikebreakers. Perhaps they feared for their own safety, or perhaps they supported the strike. Either way, they offered to surrender their badges. With the police force stretched thin, they were instead assigned to other duties. But when the riots were quelled, the superintendent of police charged all 33 with insubordination and disobedience of orders. Their jobs were at risk.

The following week, the Board of Public Safety held a trial for the officers, interviewing dozens of witnesses. The officers contended that the superintendent had asked for *volunteers* to ride the streetcars, and they had simply declined to volunteer. But the bombshell moment of the hearing came when Mayor Lew Shank defended the officers. "I wouldn't give an order to any man to do something that I would not do, and I would not have ridden one of those damn cars for the whole damn streetcar system," he testified. Now the officers could argue that they were following orders—the orders of the mayor, who had the authority to take charge of the police department during times of riot.

In the end, all of the officers were acquitted, and the superintendent of police resigned in a huff. Mayor Shank was then threatened with impeachment, and he resigned just four weeks before the end of his term. But he landed on his feet; he already had a contract to do a humorous lecture series on the vaudeville circuit.

Indianapolis mayor Lew Shank
Courtesy of the Library of Congress

Pharmacists or Bootleggers?

Brothers Louis and Julius Haag opened their first drugstore in Indianapolis in 1876, and soon they had established a winning business model—low prices with high volume. By the early 1900s, they had four stores downtown, open 7 a.m. to 11 p.m., seven days a week. The two brothers were upstanding, respected members of their community . . . until they went to prison, that is.

On May 4, 1920, the two brothers were arrested on federal charges of illegally importing alcohol into the state. The government alleged that, within a three-month period in 1918, they had brought in more than 3,300 gallons of whiskey, 385 gallons of wine, and 10 gallons of gin. The Haag brothers did not deny it. But they asserted that the alcohol was for medicinal purposes only, and was sold only when the customer had a valid doctor's prescription.

The prosecutor pointed out that many of these prescriptions—nearly 600 of them—had come from the same doctor, and he accused the Haag brothers of being in cahoots with the doctor to boost alcohol sales. For example, an unusually high number of prescriptions was written on Christmas Eve.

"Didn't you think it was unusual for so much whiskey to be sold on the night before Christmas?" the prosecutor asked at one point. The brothers stuck by their story, but the jury didn't buy it. The Haags were convicted on 29 federal counts of bootlegging and conspiracy, fined $10,600 each, and sentenced to 18 months in federal prison.

In a separate trial, the brothers were found guilty on state charges of operating a "vicious" blind tiger—a place where alcohol was sold illegally. In that case, the brothers were each sentenced to 30 days in the state penitentiary.

Courtesy of the Indiana Historical Society

The Haag brothers went to federal prison on July 31, 1920, and were paroled in February of the following year. Later that month, they entered the penal farm in Greencastle to serve their state sentences. Unfortunately, the ordeal seems to have impaired their health. Julius died in May 1922, and Louis died in June 1923 after a year-long illness. The drugstore chain stayed in the family for six more years.

Our Homegrown Gangster

Around noon on September 6, 1933, two armed men walked into the Massachusetts Avenue State Bank in Indianapolis. One held the employees and customers at gunpoint. The other leaped over the counter and forced a teller to take him to the vault. "This is a holdup, and we mean business," he said. He seized several bags of money from the vault—$24,800 in total—and then the two men fled. One of those men was John Dillinger.

Courtesy of the FBI

No story of Indianapolis crime would be complete without Dillinger, who was born here in 1903 and grew up on the East Side. During the Great Depression, the notorious gangster terrorized the Midwest, robbing banks and even raiding police armories for guns and ammunition.

Dillinger's first recorded crime was an auto theft in July 1923, after which he briefly joined the Navy, then deserted. The following year, he began his criminal career in earnest with the attempted robbery of a grocery store in Mooresville. Dillinger was quickly caught, and the judge handed down an unusually harsh sentence: Dillinger spent the next nine years in prison.

An embittered Dillinger was paroled in May 1933. Within months, he and his friends had committed armed robberies in Indiana, Michigan, and Ohio. He was arrested a few weeks after the Indianapolis holdup, but friends soon helped him escape from jail. In March 1934 he was arrested again, and this time he escaped using a fake pistol he had whittled out of wood.

Then Dillinger made a mistake. As he escaped the second time, he used the sheriff's car as a getaway vehicle. He then drove to Chicago, crossing the state line in the stolen car. This triggered the involvement of the FBI. Four months later, Dillinger was gunned down by federal agents outside a movie theater in Chicago.

Considering how infamous Dillinger became, it is interesting to note that his crime spree lasted only 14 months—from May 1933 to July 1934. Along the way, he and his gang killed 10 men and wounded several others. Nevertheless, he became a folk hero, and admirers often visit his grave at Crown Hill Cemetery.

FUGITIVE DESERVES DEATH IMMEDIATELY

John Dillinger is a danger which should immediately be done away with, said fifty-two students out of 143 in a recent poll conducted by Mr. Paul Seehausen, of the history department.

Four questions were submitted to various history classes and the students were to indicate which of the four most nearly coincided with their own opinion. Twenty-seven believed that Dillinger was so clever in his escape that he deserved his freedom. Fifty-nine others said that he should be caught, tried, and punished; five thought that since he is so keen and clever he should be regarded practically as a hero.

As the answers were turned in unsigned they represent fairly accurately the feelings of all the classes from freshmen to seniors.

A March 1934 edition of the Shortridge High School *Daily Echo* revealed mixed feelings about Dillinger.

Courtesy the Indianapolis Public Library

Courtesy of Wikimedia Commons

The Marjorie Jackson Murder

In a four-month period in the spring of 1976, Marjorie V. Jackson systematically withdrew her entire fortune—about $9 million—from Indiana National Bank. A bank employee had embezzled more than $700,000 from her accounts, and she decided her money would be safer with her, at her home on Spring Mill Road. She hauled the cash home in shopping bags and suitcases.

Word of her treasure trove spread quickly. In May of that year, she was robbed of $800,000 in cash and jewelry, but she declined to press charges or even acknowledge the theft. The following May, Howard Willard and Manuel Lee Robinson came to the house on two separate nights, robbing Jackson of millions. On the second night, Willard killed her. Then they started a fire in an attempt to destroy the evidence.

The fire was quickly extinguished, however, and the firefighters found Jackson's body much sooner than it would have been discovered otherwise. Police later found more than $5 million in cash stashed in toolboxes, trash cans, and vacuum cleaner bags around her home. They also found hoarded groceries, cakes with the message "To God, from Marjorie" written in icing, and several thousand objects wrapped in tinfoil, with cards reading, "To Jesus Christ from Marjorie Jackson."

Unsurprisingly, the case became a media sensation. It was reported that the heist was one of the largest burglaries in US history, though it was difficult to know exactly how much had been stolen.

Arrests soon followed, thanks to "almost incredible blundering" by the suspects, including large purchases made with cash still in its bank wrappers, with sequential serial numbers that could be traced to Jackson's bank account. Ultimately, Willard was convicted of murder and sentenced to life in prison. Robinson was found not guilty of murder and armed robbery, but he was convicted of six felonies, including burglary, arson, and conspiracy, and he was sentenced to 10 to 20 years in prison.

The Burger Chef Murders

Late on the night of November 17, 1978, Brian King drove past the Burger Chef where he worked on Crawfordsville Road in Speedway. He wasn't scheduled to work that night, but he noticed that the lights were still on, so he decided to stop by and say hello. He found the back door open, the cash registers and office ransacked, and the closing crew missing, having left their jackets and purses behind. He called 911.

The next day, the closing crew's bodies were found in a heavily wooded area in nearby Johnson County. One victim, Daniel Davis, was 16 years old and a junior at Decatur Central High School. He'd been moved to the closing crew only the previous week. Ruth Ellen Shelton, 17, was a junior at Northwest High School, an honors student who planned to study computer science. She had already turned in her resignation from the restaurant, but the manager had persuaded her to stay a few extra weeks while he trained a replacement. Davis and Shelton

Courtesy of Bass Photo Co. Collection, Indiana Historical Society

both died of multiple gunshot wounds. Mark Flemmonds, also 16, was a sophomore at Speedway High School. The short-order cook wasn't scheduled to work that night, but he'd switched shifts with a co-worker who needed the night off. He died of blunt force trauma. Jayne Friedt, 20, was the assistant manager working that night. A graduate of Avon High School, she was about to be promoted to manager, but she didn't know that. She was stabbed twice with a hunting knife. The gruesome details are included here as a reminder that these were people—children, really—and not just names in the headlines.

The police treated the case as a robbery gone wrong. They pursued many leads over the years—making plenty of mistakes along the way—but the case remains unsolved.

The Speedway Bombings

For the Speedway community, 1978 was a weird year. In September, eight bombs were planted around town—in trash cans, in vacant lots, and even under the car of an off-duty police officer. Police later arrested a man named Brett Kimberlin, alleging that he set off the bombs to distract the police from investigating a murder he had committed that July. He was later convicted on 22 counts.

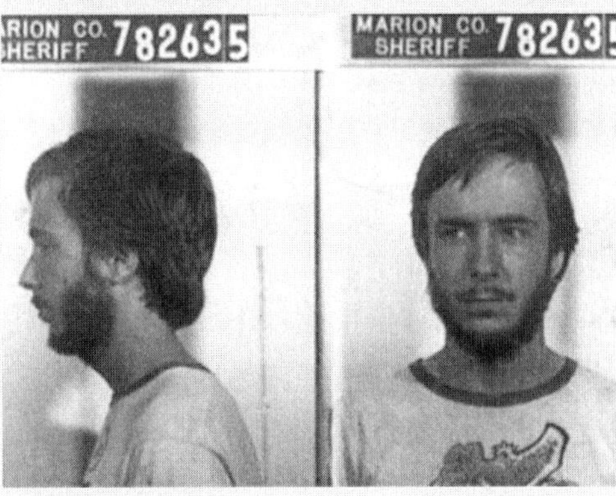

Brett Kimberlin
Courtesy of Marion County Sheriff's Office

The Kiritsis Hostage Crisis

In 1977, an Indianapolis man named Tony Kiritsis uncovered a conspiracy to ruin him—or so he thought. Several years earlier, he had taken out a commercial loan for $110,000 to develop a piece of property on the West Side. Although the loan had been extended several times and even increased, Kiritsis was certain the mortgage company, Meridian Mortgage, was working against him because it wanted the land for itself. So, Kiritsis took a hostage, and in doing so ignited a debate that still rages today. Was Kiritsis a common criminal or a modern folk hero standing up for the little guy?

On the morning of February 8, 1977, Kiritsis arrived at the Meridian Mortgage office for a meeting with the president, Richard Hall. Hall was under the impression that Kiritsis wanted him to look at site development plans. But when Hall's back was turned, Kiritsis pulled a gun. He wired the barrel of a shotgun to the back of Hall's neck, rigging it with a dead man's line. Then he called 911 to announce his actions.

"In my entire life, I had never seen a man as wild-eyed as Tony Kiritsis was at that moment," Hall later wrote in a book about

Courtesy of SimmeD, Wikimedia Commons

the incident. "And my first thought was that I couldn't understand how God would let a man get that angry."

Kiritsis then commandeered a police car and forced Hall to drive them to Kiritsis's apartment. The hostage crisis lasted for 63 hours and became a media circus. Kiritsis called local radio stations to air his grievances and make his demands. He wanted immunity from prosecution, he wanted his loan to be forgiven, and he wanted Meridian Mortgage to admit the many ways it had wronged him. The crisis culminated in a live press conference, which Kiritsis attended with Hall still attached to the shotgun. Local and national television stations aired the event while worrying that they were about to broadcast a murder.

Fortunately for Hall, Kiritsis believed the FBI's false promises that his demands would be met, and after the press conference he surrendered. He later was found not guilty by reason of insanity—a verdict that prompted significant changes in state law related to insanity defenses.

Our Homegrown Serial Killer

In the winter of 1995, three children were playing in the woods behind their home in Hamilton County when they came across a human skeleton. They shared the discovery with their mother, who gave police permission to search the rest of their property, called Fox Hollow Farm. There, a forensic anthropologist eventually identified more than 10,000 bones and bone fragments from an estimated 25 murder victims. A few years earlier, young men had started to go missing from gay clubs in downtown Indianapolis. Using DNA testing, investigators soon linked those cases to the bodies found at Fox Hollow Farm—and to the farm's owner, Herb Baumeister.

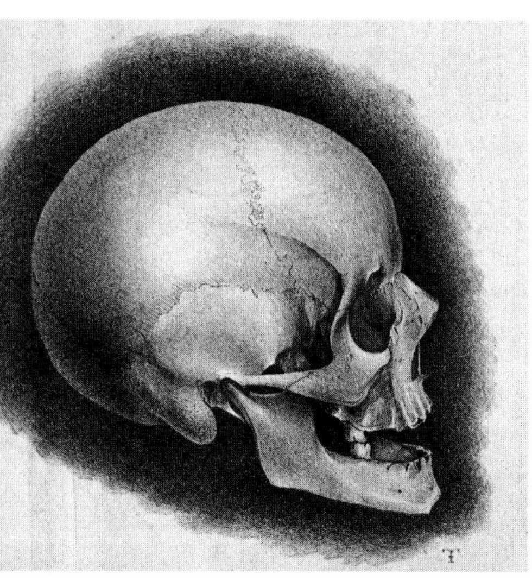

Courtesy of Wellcome Collection

Baumeister was born in Indianapolis in 1947; he grew up in the Butler-Tarkington neighborhood and attended North Central High School. As an adult, he and his wife founded a chain of Sav-A-Lot thrift stores. In 1991, that success enabled them to purchase the farm, a secluded 18-acre estate off 156th Street and the Monon Trail. When his family was away, police alleged, Baumeister lured men back to the indoor swimming pool at his home, where he strangled them.

Police also linked Baumeister to a series of murders along I-70 between Indianapolis and Columbus, Ohio. In the 1980s, nine young men, partially nude, were found dumped in shallow streams along the interstate. The pattern stopped just as Baumeister and his wife were buying Fox Hollow Farm.

Baumeister was never formally named as a suspect in the murders. He was never arrested and never charged with a crime. He was away from home when the discovery at his farm became national news, and he fled to Canada. There, he died by suicide. He left behind a three-page letter that made no mention of the murders, but he did apologize for spoiling the scenery at the park where he died. As recently as 2024, investigators were still using the bone fragments found at the farm to identify additional victims.

The Devil Comes to Irvington

Serial killer H. H. Holmes—of *Devil in the White City* fame—committed most of his crimes in Chicago, but he also lived briefly in the 5800 block of Julian Avenue in Irvington. There he killed a young boy, Howard Pitzel, the son of his former partner in crime. Holmes burned the body and stuffed it up the chimney flue, where it was later discovered by three boys playing detective. The house is allegedly haunted.

Courtesy of Wikimedia Commons

The Kmart Toothpaste Bomb

Louis Profeta, a third-year medical student, was shopping at a Castleton-area Kmart one evening in April 1989 when he heard what sounded like "a giant balloon" popping. Thinking it might have been a gunshot, he rushed toward the sound as everyone else rushed away. In the aisle of garbage bags, he found smoke and debris—and a small child, who was on fire and bleeding profusely.

Courtesy of Wikimedia Commons and Miami 9918

The child was 5-year-old Erin Bower, a kindergartner. Bower had noticed a container of toothpaste out of place among the trash bags, and she had picked it up. It was a homemade pipe bomb. The blast severed most of her left hand, and there was shrapnel in her left eye. She was stabilized at the scene by Profeta and an off-duty firefighter, who improvised medical equipment from the housewares within reach. At the hospital, surgeons were unable to save the hand, which was amputated. Bower eventually lost her left eye, as well. The event received extensive media coverage, and parents across the nation were terrified.

Meanwhile, teenager David L. Swinford was at home discussing the incident with his family. Someone said, "What a terrible person must have done this," and Swinford replied, "I'm sure whoever did it didn't mean to hurt a little girl." Swinford died by suicide 36 hours after the blast. In his possession police found the tools and materials used to create the bomb, including BBs and the wires from Christmas tree lights. "If he did do it, I can see why he committed suicide," his mother later said. "That little girl looks exactly like his 4-year-old sister."

In 2018, Bower, her husband, and her parents attended the retirement party of John Moriarty, the off-duty firefighter who had helped Profeta save her life. By then Bower was 34, and she had become a pediatric physical therapist. "I knew I wanted to help children," she said, "and I wanted to be in health care."

The MARMON

"The Easiest Riding Car in the World"

The Marmon "Thirty-Two" Touring Car

$2,400.00

Manufactured by

NORDYKE & MARMON COMPANY

INDIANAPOLIS, INDIANA

Established 1851

Chapter Four

Lost Industries

You may know that Indianapolis once had a booming automotive industry, but did you know it was once a center for bicycle manufacturing, as well? And have you heard of the Columbia Conserve Company, which was once famous worldwide for its democratic management approach? If not, this chapter is for you; it celebrates the companies we have lost. Also included are stories about a trio of dazzling amusement parks, the company that manufactured the world's largest drum, a major publishing house, and one of the largest breweries in the nation. Nostalgic readers will fondly remember the tale of L. S. Ayres, but this chapter also covers the devastating downfall of local icon Roselyn Bakeries. Although these companies are no longer with us, they played an integral part in the Circle City's growth and development.

The Coney Island of the Midwest

In May 1906, children across Indianapolis must have begged their parents for extra pocket money. Three separate amusement parks opened in the city that month, celebrating a dazzling modern era of electrification and mechanization.

First came the grand re-opening of Riverside Amusement Park. It had opened three years previously, in 1903, but had undergone a major renovation. It re-opened on May 6 and featured a roller coaster, mirror maze, aerial swing, scenic river, miniature railway, and bowling alley. It also offered canoe rentals for outings on the White River.

Next up was Wonderland Amusement Park, which opened May 19 to a crowd of about 8,000. It was "a topsy-turvy fantasy world of both natural and mechanical amusement," one historian wrote, and it had about 50,000 electric lights. The main feature was the 125-foot-tall Electric Tower, but the park also had a treetop scenic railway, a bumpy slide, a "mystic maze," a bandshell, and its very own elephant.

Nine days later, on May 28, the White City Amusement Park opened in Broad Ripple. This park had a Coney Island-style boardwalk, a re-creation of the Pompeii volcano disaster, a roller coaster, a roller-skating rink, a dance pavilion, a soda fountain, a bandstand with live music, and a restaurant. Although it seems bizarre now, White City also had an exhibit of preemie babies in incubators.

Unsurprisingly, the competition was intense. For the 1907 season, Wonderland added a monkey house with 48 residents, and Riverside added a Wild West show with trained monkeys. In 1908, Wonderland added a restaurant with free vaudeville entertainment, and White City debuted its new bathing beach and added an alligator show (which was *not* at the bathing beach).

But the heyday of Indy amusement parks was short-lived. White City was destroyed by fire in 1908, and the property is now Broad Ripple Park. Wonderland infuriated the community in 1909 by applying for a liquor license, and business dropped so dramatically that the park closed to the public, remaining open only for group rentals and fundraising events. It burned in 1911. Riverside, the first of the three to open, outlasted its competition and survived until 1970.

The Electric Tower at Wonderland Amusement Park

The Hoosier House

New York City has long been the center of the US publishing industry, but Indianapolis once had a powerhouse publisher of its own. Nicknamed the "Hoosier House," Bobbs-Merrill launched the careers of many Indiana authors and published some of the best-selling books of the 20th century.

Bobbs-Merrill got its start in 1850, when attorney Samuel Merrill co-founded the publishing house of Hood & Merrill. A second ancestor, the Bowen line, was founded in 1853, and both companies published their first books in 1855. After a long series of mergers, the two lines joined to form Bowen-Merrill in 1885, and the company changed its name to Bobbs-Merrill in 1903.

Bobbs-Merrill brought the world *The Fountainhead* by Ayn Rand; *The Joy of Cooking* by Irma S. Rombauer; books by William Styron, Vladimir Nabokov, and Nikki Giovanni; and the first American edition of *The Phantom of the Opera*. It also published *The New Wizard of Oz* by L. Frank Baum, which for many years was the best-selling children's book in America. Another success was the Childhood of Famous Americans series, which grew to include more than 200 biographies for young readers. The company published numerous books by the "Hoosier poet," James Whitcomb Riley. And it was also one of the world's largest publishers of law books.

Other Bobbs-Merrill books that were best-sellers at the time have since faded from memory. The company's first best-seller was 1898's *When Knighthood Was in Flower* by Charles Major. It also published Hoosier author Meredith Nicholson's *The House of a Thousand Candles*, the #4 fiction best-seller of 1906. Three years later it published Mary Roberts Rinehart's *The Man in Lower Ten*, the first American detective story to make the best-seller list. Rinehart was one of the most popular

American writers of the early 20th century. In 1926, Bobbs-Merrill published the #1 best-sellers of the year in both fiction (*The Private Life of Helen of Troy*) and nonfiction (*The Man Nobody Knows: A Discovery of the Real Jesus*). Several of the company's books went on to win Pulitzer Prizes in fiction, biography, and drama.

Despite those successes, in 1958 the company became a subsidiary of Howard W. Sams & Co., which was later purchased by the International Telephone & Telegraph Company. Macmillan purchased ITT in 1985, and it dissolved Bobbs-Merrill later that year.

Courtesy of Bass Photo Co. Collection, Indiana Historical Society

Wagons and Wheels

Transportation has always been a major industry in Indianapolis. It is, after all, the "crossroads of America." So, before Hoosiers had automobiles, and before racecars zoomed around the Indianapolis Motor Speedway, the city was home to major manufacturers of both wagons and wheels.

Founded in Rushville, the Parry Manufacturing Company moved to Indianapolis in 1886. Its first specialty was two-wheeled road carts, and in 1890 the company began to manufacture four-wheeled carriages, such as surreys and phaetons. The company had "the established reputation for making the very best goods for the smallest amount of money," wrote Max R. Hyman in the 1897 edition of *Hyman's Hand Book of Indianapolis.* So, the company "invaded the field occupied by the oldest and strongest carriage manufacturers." At the time, the Parry facility was larger than the nation's next five carriage factories put together, it employed 2,800 people, and it was churning out 350 four-wheel carts every day.

Meanwhile, the Woodburn Sarven Wheel Company was founded in 1847 to manufacture shoemaker's instruments. The company later acquired the patent to the "celebrated Sarven patent wheel," and business boomed. The wheel was superior to others because it had joints reinforced with iron. In 1870, a historian wrote that the company was now "making wheels of all kinds, from those for the lightest buggy, weighing no more than 80 pounds, to those for heavy omnibuses and wagons." By 1884 the factory was the largest establishment of its kind in the nation, and perhaps the world.

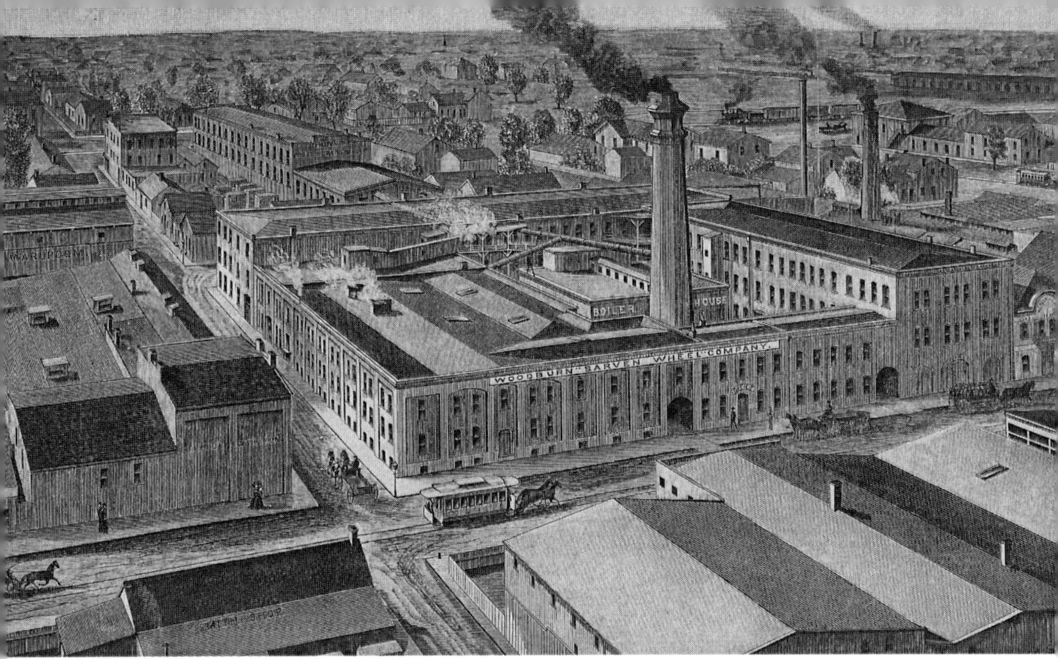

In 1890, these two behemoths of transportation merged. The Woodburn Sarven Wheel Company was purchased by Parry, which no doubt incorporated the patented wheel into its carriage designs. Parry survived until 1919, but by then its products had been replaced by a newer innovation in transportation: the automobile.

The Supreme Sacrifice

The first Indianapolis fireman to die in the line of duty was Daniel Glazier, chief fire engineer, in 1873. He was fighting a fire at the Woodburn Sarven Wheel Company when he was buried beneath a falling wall. Glazier's funeral was one of the largest the city had ever seen, and two of his sons went on to become firemen.

Bicycle Manufacturing

A revolution in transportation occurred in the 1880s. High-wheel bicycles were already available, but they were dangerous and difficult to manage. Then a man in England, John Kemp Starley, invented what he called a "safety" bicycle, similar to the ones we use today. A few years later, a man named John Boyd Dunlop patented the pneumatic tire. "The combination of these two improvements led to a huge and sudden increase in the demand for bicycles in Europe and America," one historian wrote. And Indianapolis was at the forefront of the emerging industry.

In 1895, a national cycling magazine wrote that "no city excels Indianapolis in the magnitude of its bicycle industry." By that time, bicycle shops and riding schools lined the west side of Pennsylvania Street from Market to Ohio. L. S. Ayres advertised its cycling clothes and accessories, and the Zig-Zag Cycling Club organized group rides. Meanwhile, Indy native Major Taylor—future world champion—was starting to win bicycle races across the nation.

That year Indy was home to nine bicycle manufacturers, some of which earned a national reputation. The 1897 edition of *Hyman's Hand Book of Indianapolis* noted the Hay & Willits Manufacturing Company, which was expected to made 5,000 of its Outing bicycles that year. It also highlighted Central Cycle Manufacturing Co., which made the popular Ben-Hur line of bicycles. "Today the plant is one of the most important of the many industrial institutions in our city," the book stated. "The sale of the 'Ben-Hur' bicycles is increasing with their growing popularity, and these famous wheels find a market all over the world." Meanwhile, the Indiana Bicycle Company manufactured the well-known Waverley, and the Diamond Chain Company—which survived for more than a century—was founded in Indianapolis to manufacture bicycle drive chains.

The cycling frenzy was short-lived, petering out after the turn of the century. But the industry had created a deep bench of mechanics and engineers in Indianapolis—one reason the city was such a successful hub for auto manufacturing in the early 1900s.

Courtesy of the Indiana Pamphlet Collection, Indiana Division, Indiana State Library

Early Auto Manufacturing

When the Indianapolis Motor Speedway was built in 1909, races like the Indianapolis 500 were an afterthought. The primary purpose of the facility was to serve as a test track for Indiana's booming auto industry, which at the time was larger than even Michigan's. By 1920, more than 200 makes of automobile were manufactured in Indiana, many of them in Indianapolis. In particular, the city was known for its luxury brands, such as Cole, Marmon, Stutz, and Duesenberg.

Joseph Cole, a carriage manufacturer, turned his attention to cars in 1908. By 1912 the Cole Motor Car Company was producing 2,000 cars per year, primarily in competition with Cadillac. The vehicles sold for $2,500 at a time when a Ford Model T cost just $550.

The Marmon was one of the most successful local brands, ultimately selling more than 100,000 units. It was produced by a division of

Nordyke & Marmon, which primarily manufactured machinery for flour mills. One of the company's racecars, the Marmon Wasp, was victorious at the first Indy 500 in 1911.

Like Marmon, Harry C. Stutz's Ideal Motor Car Company made its name in racing. The company built a racecar in five weeks to compete in the first Indy 500, where it placed 11th and became known as "the car that made good in a day." The company's most famous model was the Bearcat, one of the earliest sports cars.

The most elegant of all was the Duesenberg, which dominated racing in the 1920s. Fewer than 500 of the cars were ever manufactured, and today they are the holy grail of classic car collecting. In 2018, a Duesenberg SSJ from 1935 sold at auction for $22 million, a new record.

By 1924, the price of a Ford Model T had dropped to just $265, and Indy's luxury auto companies found it difficult to compete. Cole liquidated in 1925, and for the other companies the Great Depression was fatal. But the speedway still stands as a testament to Indy's early dominance in auto manufacturing.

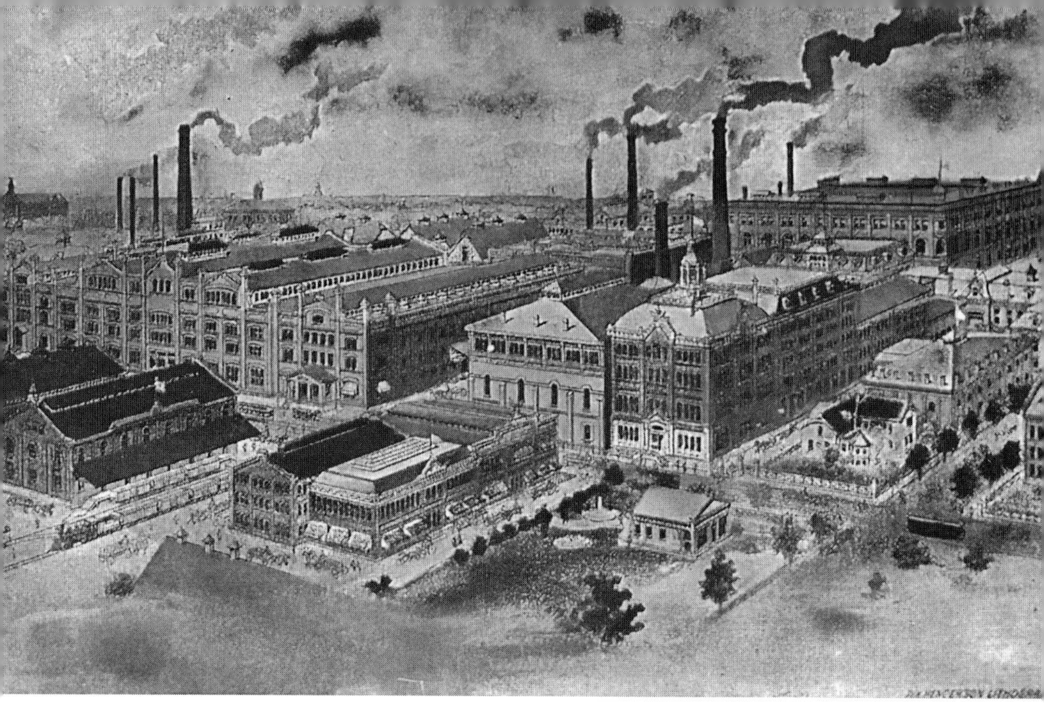
Courtesy of the Indiana Historical Society

Indianapolis Brewing Company

By the 1940s, the Indianapolis Brewing Company could trace its history back to 1859. It had survived the Civil War, Prohibition, and two world wars, and it seemed poised for continued success. But then the IRS came to call.

As in most US cities, the brewery business in early Indianapolis was dominated by German immigrants and their descendants. In 1859, just one year after a statewide alcohol ban was struck down as unconstitutional, Christian Frederick Schmidt co-founded the city's first successful brewery. Four years later, in 1863, Peter Lieber and two others bought a brewery called Gagg & Co. And two years after that, Casper Maus & Co. opened a brewery on West New York Street. Now skip ahead to 1889, when the three breweries merged to form the Indianapolis Brewing Company.

For a time, the IBC was managed by Albert Lieber, the grandfather of Indianapolis writer Kurt Vonnegut. The brewery was best known for its Duesseldorfer beer, which won a gold medal at the Paris Exposition in 1900 and the grand prize at the Louisiana Purchase Exposition in 1904. By then the brewery employed 1,200 people and was one of the 10 largest breweries in the nation. It survived Prohibition by manufacturing sodas, malt extracts, and medicinal tonics.

However, the brewery's success ended abruptly in 1947. The company was accused of under-filling its beer bottles and thus making excess profit. The IRS handed the company a bill for $1.1 million in damages and unpaid taxes. It was far more than the company was worth. The brewery went into receivership, and production was halted that October. A year later, the brewery sold for just $105,000, and the new owner made plans to convert the building into warehouse space.

Indiana's Alcohol Laws

Historically, Indiana has had strict laws related to alcohol. The General Assembly enacted a statewide alcohol ban in 1855, which the Indiana Supreme Court later declared unconstitutional. Indiana went dry again in 1918, meaning Prohibition started here two years early. In 1923, Indiana became the first state in the nation to pass a law against drunk driving.

Courtesy of the National Cancer Institute

An Experiment in Democracy

More than a century ago, the Columbia Conserve Company of Indianapolis launched a dramatic experiment in workplace democracy. Although it is now largely forgotten, the company earned international recognition at the time for its innovations, which were far ahead of their time.

Founded in 1903, the Columbia Conserve Company manufactured canned goods in its Beech Grove facility. The business nearly failed in 1910, then barely held on until 1916, the first year it turned a significant profit. Meanwhile, the company president, William Powers Hapgood, was becoming increasingly uncomfortable with his leadership role.

"I realized how empty is the American dogma that merit is always recognized," he later wrote. "In my own case, I knew that it was not mainly, or even chiefly, through ability that I held my place." Rather, he held his position because he had money. He wrote, "I felt confident that within the ranks of the workers there must be a vast store of ability which would rapidly develop if exposed to a favorable atmosphere."

In 1917, Hapgood announced a new way of running the business. Decisions would be made, not by management staff, but by a majority vote of a workers' council. Hapgood's experiment also included a profit-sharing plan, as well as a stock-purchase plan that gradually led to employee ownership.

Under the council's direction, the company began offering benefits that seem common to us today, but were radical at the time. All employees were shifted from uncertain hourly wages to a guaranteed annual salary, and the workweek was reduced from 55 hours to 50. The company also began to offer free health care, paid vacations, retirement pensions, and educational benefits. During the Great Depression, the workers—by their own choice—all took large pay cuts so that nobody would be laid off.

Courtesy of the Indiana Historical Society

The experiment lasted until 1942, when a series of worker strikes, lawsuits, and counter-lawsuits dissolved the trust that held company stock in common for all workers. The courts resolved the mess, and in 1953 the company was sold. Nevertheless, for decades the company had proved it was possible to treat employees fairly while still turning a profit.

The World Makers

Chances are, the globes and pull-down maps in your childhood classrooms were manufactured right here in Indianapolis. For decades, the city was home to the George F. Cram Company, the second-largest producer of globes in the world.

The company's founder, George F. Cram, got his start in map-making as a topographer in the Union army during the Civil War. In 1867 he and his uncle, Rufus Blanchard, started a map business in Evanston, Illinois. Two years later Cram took over the company and renamed it after himself. For decades, the company's best-selling product was *Cram's Unrivaled Family Atlas of the World.*

The company remained in Illinois until the 1920s, when it was acquired by Indy's National Map Company. The George F. Cram name was well known, so the merged organization kept that name but moved all operations to Indianapolis. Soon after, in 1932, the company added globes to its product line—from standard classroom globes of the Earth to moon globes and globe lamps illuminated from within. It also manufactured globes in Spanish, French, and Hebrew. And it made special mounts for the globes based on trends in interior design.

The company grew steadily in the following decades. "When dictators go on a rampage, sales skyrocket for mapmakers," read a 1951 *Indianapolis Star* profile of the company. Globe and map sales spiked during WWII and the Korean War because families wanted to follow the troop movements of their loved ones.

"I am sorry that we are the beneficiaries of a war demand," said company president E. A. Peterson at the time. "But the public wants information, and that's what we supply."

By 1955, when the *Star* again profiled the George F. Cram Company, it was the oldest map manufacturer in the United States. Loren B. Douthit purchased the company in 1966, and under his leadership business tripled, largely because of a stronger emphasis on retail sales.

Despite more than a century of success, it was impossible for the company to compete with the internet and its instant access to information. The Douthit family sold the company to Herff Jones in 2005, and in 2012 the product line was discontinued.

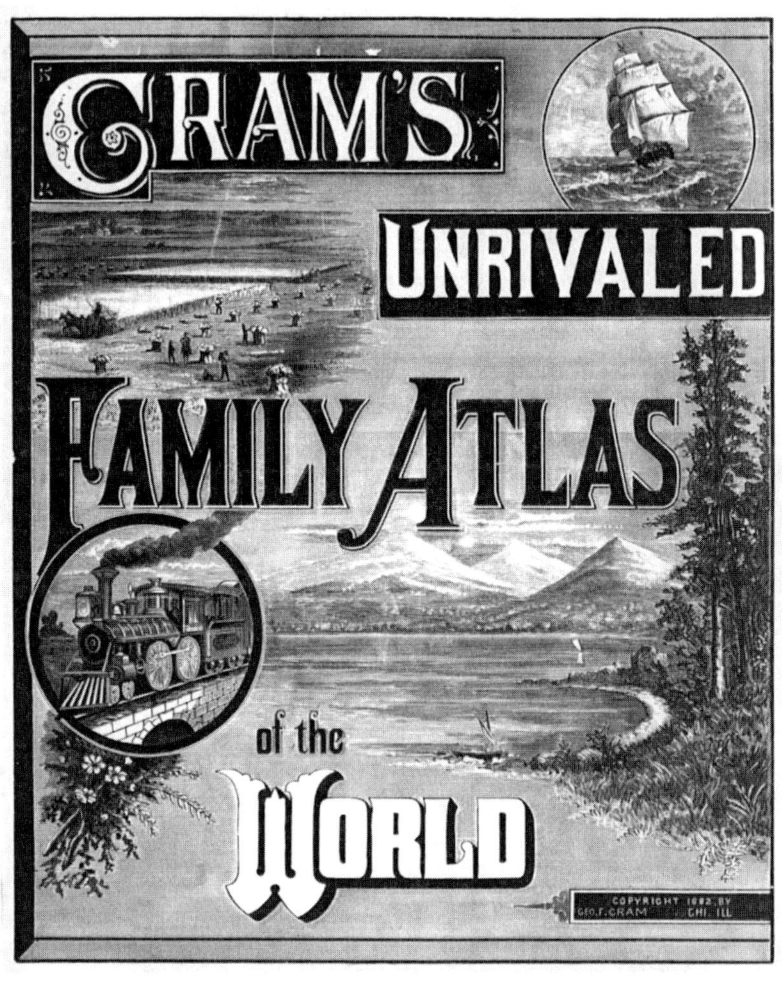

Courtesy of the Bass Photo Co. Collection, Indiana Historical Society

Drumroll, Please

Between 1903 and 1930, Indianapolis was home to the largest manufacturer of percussion instruments in the world. The Leedy Manufacturing Company was best known for building Purdue University's bass drum, billed as the largest in the world. But generations of drummers knew Leedy for its meticulous workmanship.

In the 1890s, Ulysses G. Leedy was a trap drummer for the orchestra at English's Opera House when he decided he could build a better instrument. He made a drum for himself, then more drums for other musicians, and soon he had more orders than he could handle. In 1898, Leedy moved the operation out of his apartment into a dedicated space in the Cyclorama building; in 1903, when the building was demolished, he moved the factory to the northeast corner of Palmer Street and

Barth Avenue. The factory produced every part of every instrument and thus had a tannery, lumberyard, chrome-plating works, and so on. In all, the company produced more than 900 types of instruments and accessories. Among them was the world's first vibraphone.

In the 1920s, the company's growth was fueled by the popularity of jazz and the new drum and bugle corps being formed by WWI veterans. In 1928, the company expected sales of $2 million, employed about 200 people, and used 225,000 calf skins. Its authorized dealers were spread across the globe.

"Hardly an orchestra plays in a motion picture house, a theater, or concert hall, and hardly a band plays in a park or marches in the streets in the United States that does not have some kind of Leedy instrument in it," reported the *Indianapolis News.*

Unfortunately, Leedy himself was in failing health, and he sold the company to a competitor, C. G. Conn Ltd., in 1929. Within a year, manufacturing operations were moved to Elkhart, Indiana. The Leedy brand name was used on drums well into the 1960s, but Leedy himself died of heart disease soon after the sale, in 1931.

The Electric Vibraphone

Sometime in the 1920s, company vice president Herman Winterhoff invented a new instrument—the electric vibraphone. Picture a scaled-up xylophone. A tubular resonator was positioned beneath each aluminum bar, and electric fans placed in between the bars and resonators created a vibrato effect. The instrument soon caught on with jazz and dance bands.

An overhead view of a vibraphone
Courtesy of Wikimedia Commons

L. S. Ayres

In the early decades of the 20th century, the L. S. Ayres department store was a retail wonderland. It stocked the usual housewares and ready-to-wear fashions, but it also had a soda fountain, bookstore, salon, bakery, and grocery—not to mention its beloved fifth-floor tea room. Most importantly, its dressmaking department was at one time the largest in the nation.

L. S. Ayres was founded in 1851, when H. A. Fletcher & Co. opened a department store in Indianapolis with a "large stock of goods bought in New York and Boston." After a series of moves and ownership changes, it relaunched as the Trade Palace in 1867, with dry goods on the first floor and carpets upstairs. In 1872, Lyman Ayres of Oswego, New York, bought a controlling interest in the store, and he soon changed the name to his own.

In 1905 the store moved to the corner of Washington and Meridian Streets, and in 1915 the store expanded. The building had modern elevators, natural light, marble and mahogany accents, and a mezzanine rest area with lavatories and writing desks. By 1919 the store had $4.5 million in annual sales and about 2,000 employees, who were meticulously trained.

Over the years, L. S. Ayres developed a reputation for "strictly high-class" goods. "Nothing shoddy or worthless is ever to be found on our counters," read an advertisement in March 1878. Modern women's fashions were a particular specialty. In the 1930s, the store debuted a new "That Ayres Look" advertising campaign, featuring colorful sketches of upcoming fashions.

In the 1950s, L. S. Ayres followed its customers to the suburbs, opening branches in popular shopping malls. By the 1970s, however, the downtown store was in decline. In 1972 the company was sold to the Associated Dry Goods Company, which was acquired by May Department Stores in 1986. In turn, May was acquired by Federated Department Stores, which owned Macy's. The L. S. Ayres brand survived until 2006, when the eight remaining stores were converted to Macy's locations.

Courtesy of the Library of Congress

The Downfall of Roselyn Bakeries

It's hard to imagine a more disastrous fall from grace than Roselyn Bakeries. The beloved local company served Indy's sweet tooth for half a century, but in the end, it left its customers both disappointed and disgusted.

The bakery was founded in 1943 by John S. Clark Jr. and his wife, Mildred. Within five years, it had opened two more locations. In 1950 the company launched a wholesale operation, selling its baked goods directly to grocery stores. To accommodate that demand, the company moved all of its baking operations to a central kitchen at 30th and Keystone. This facility would be the company's downfall.

In 1999, the Marion County Public Health Department received complaints about unsanitary conditions at the bakery, and it conducted an unannounced inspection that June. Inspectors cited 41 violations of health and safety standards, calling the facility "probably the worst they had ever seen." The table used for cutting brownies was covered with dead insects. Inspectors found "gross accumulations" of dust, dirt, food debris, grease, and insects on the bakery equipment. They also found rodent tracks and fresh rodent droppings, swarms of gnats, stagnant water, filthy floors and ceilings, and bird feathers. "We informed them that these items had to be corrected immediately," one health inspector said. When inspectors returned the following week and found the issues unresolved, they shut the facility down.

By then Roselyn had nearly 40 stores throughout Central Indiana, and that weekend all of them were closed—and the public soon knew why. Four days later, the freshly cleaned central kitchen was back up and

Courtesy of the Indiana Historical Society

running, with Health Department approval, but customers no longer trusted the bakery.

On July 8, the company published an open letter from CEO Jeffrey Clark. "There are no excuses for the circumstances" that led to the closure, he wrote, and he apologized for the "great deal of inconvenience." He added, "You have my personal assurance that every Roselyn product we bake is, and will continue to be, safe, fresh, and of the highest quality."

The public appeal was futile. A month later, the company ceased operations, citing the "exhaustive adverse media publicity" it had received.

Harry Houdini escapes from a giant milk can filled with water.
Courtesy of the Library of Congress

Chapter Five

Pure Weirdness

This chapter was especially fun to write. It starts with the Great Squirrel Invasion of 1822 and ends with a volunteer "snake hostess." In between, you'll find stories of ridiculous theater performances, quack doctors, and bizarre publicity stunts. You'll read about the Irvington School War, the Indianapolis antics of Harry Houdini, the disaster of the *Robert Hanna*, and the city's first recorded exorcism. The strange downfall of a vice president is covered here, as is the "family" that became a poster child for the eugenics movement nationwide. This chapter also discusses the mysterious curse of the governor's mansion, as well as a massive prank that fooled everyone, including the media. Curses, exorcisms, a shipwreck, and some squirrels—what more could you want from a chapter?

The Great Squirrel Invasion of 1822

Farming was a challenge for early settlers in Indianapolis. In the city's first year, a malaria epidemic sickened all but three people in town; nobody was available to tend the crops, and a lean winter ensued. The following year seemed much more promising—that is, until a plague of squirrels descended on the city. The event came to be known as the Great Squirrel Invasion of 1822.

"The corn this year was literally destroyed . . . by grey and black squirrels," wrote settler Calvin Fletcher in a letter to his brother. "There was one man killed around one cornfield 248 [squirrels] in three days." Another man reported killing 18 squirrels from a tree without changing position or missing a shot.

"They came from nowhere by the tens of thousands, swimming the White River and descending upon the village like a plague of locusts," wrote historian Edward A. Leary. "They were everywhere: in the trees, grass, fields, and gardens; in the cabins, under beds, in lofts and chimney corners. They devoured everything in sight."

Historian Jeannette Covert Nolan wrote, "Squirrels were in your house, under your feet, peeping wickedly at you from behind every door you opened. They were outside in the grass, sitting in the bushes, laughing their impudent laughter at you from the treetops."

The settlers spent all day patrolling their fields, trying to kill the squirrels or at least scare them away. At night, they stayed up late molding new bullets. But the squirrels didn't scare easily, because they were starving to death. For whatever reason, the trees that year hadn't produced enough nuts to sustain them. And to be fair to the squirrels, the settlers constituted an invading horde of their own. Unfortunately for the humans, the squirrels they managed to shoot were so emaciated that they weren't fit to eat. The people of Indianapolis faced yet another hungry winter, while the surviving squirrels moved on to greener pastures.

The Smiths' Theatrical Disaster

The first theatrical performance in Indianapolis took place on New Year's Eve in 1823. It featured a Mr. and Mrs. Smith, "late of the New York theater," in two plays: *Doctor's Courtship, or the Indulgent Father* and the farce *Jealous Lovers*. But the featured attraction was Mrs. Smith singing the "Star-Spangled Banner" while dancing a hornpipe, blindfolded, amongst eggs. Admission cost a quarter.

The performance was ridiculous for several reasons. First, Mr. and Mrs. Smith were ill-suited for their roles. "Both not less than 50 years of age! Representing *jealous lovers*! Lord, what a snowstorm in May and June," wrote settler Calvin Fletcher, whose diaries are a rich source of information about the city's early years.

Another sticking point was the music. The performance was held in the tavern of Thomas Carter, a strict Baptist who permitted only religious music (but who apparently had nothing against alcohol). Bill Bagwell, the local fiddler who played for the Smiths, had to convince Carter that his fiddle—an "obnoxious" instrument of sin and vice—was actually a violin. Carter was appeased when the fiddler played a hymn and promised to stick to religious tunes. "This restriction, considering the nature of the performance and the character of the players, was so extremely ludicrous that the audience was convulsed with laughter during the whole evening," one historian wrote.

Fletcher wrote in his journal, "I apologized to myself for going." But he went again the next day, "with about the sum totum of edification."

Mr. and Mrs. Smith returned to Indianapolis the following year, but a scathing newspaper review discouraged attendance. The Smiths skipped town without paying the printer for their handbills.

Falling in Love

Another ridiculous theater moment began when a Capt. George W. Cutter fell in love with the actress Mrs. Drake while they were staying at the same Indianapolis hotel. She was many years his senior, "fat, fair, and forty," but their relationship flourished nonetheless. He escorted her to the theater each night and watched from backstage. One evening, her part required her character to fall down. Cutter, thinking the fall was genuine, rushed onstage, "to the utter confusion of the scene and the uproarious delight of the audience," one historian wrote. The couple married soon afterward.

Indy's First "Exorcism"

Early Indianapolis settlers were a superstitious bunch. Hoosiers never burned any witches at the stake, but some residents still believed in the power of witchcraft to cause illness and other misfortunes.

A family named Catlin (or something similar) once lived on the southeast corner of Alabama and Washington Streets. When one of the children fell sick, the family blamed witchcraft. And the solution, they decided, was an exorcism. They sent for Dr. John L. Richmond, who was both a practicing physician and the minister of the Baptist church, and asked him to perform the rite.

Richmond thought the idea was nonsense. But he also "concluded that a remedy adapted to the faith and brains of the family would be the best he could use," wrote historian B. R. Sulgrove. In other words, he decided to fake it. In the presence of the awe-struck family, he concocted a "magic potion" made of cat hair, hog lard, and other mystical ingredients. Then he recited an incantation and threw the potion into the fireplace. The lard flared up, and when it finished burning, the darkness was complete. That's when one of Richmond's students, a Mr. Barrett, ran through the house, making a trail of beef's blood from the sick child to the front door.

Courtesy of Jose Guadalupe Posada, Metropolitan Museum of Art

Richmond told the family that the trail of blood showed "that the witch's blood had been spilt and her power was at an end." The sick child "was cured at once" due to the placebo effect of the ceremony, just as Richmond had predicted.

Early Circle City Superstitions

Many of us are superstitious about black cats, broken mirrors, and ladders, but the early settlers of Indianapolis had some unusual beliefs of their own. As historian B. R. Sulgrove wrote:

- If a boy kills a toad, his family's cow will give bloody milk.
- If a knife is dropped from the table, a visitor is coming.
- If a dog howls for a long time at night, death is coming.
- If a person pares his nails on a Sunday, he will be made ashamed of something by the end of the week.
- Killing a snake and leaving it lying belly upward brings rainfall.
- A large crop of dog fennel portends a season of sickness.

Courtesy of Wikimedia Commons

The "Indian Doctor"

The medical profession in the early years of Indianapolis was, as one historian put it, "a free-for-all." Being a doctor didn't require a license, a medical degree, or any other qualifications. If you said you were a doctor, you were. Into this situation walked Dr. Willian Kelley Frohawk Fryer, an "Indian doctor," who billed himself as "a regular graduate of Nature's wide Botanic Garden and Common Sense Medical College."

The 24-year-old naturopath was white, but he claimed to have spent a "long residence among the Indians." In 1839 he published his *Indian Guide to Health* in Indianapolis, and for a few years he ran a "Sanative House" here. He sometimes provided medical treatment in exchange for herbs, roots, and bark from the forests.

Little documentation from Fryer's time in Indianapolis survives. But around 1850 he moved to New Orleans, and his newspaper advertisements from that city reveal a lot about his methods. Fryer claimed to have cured more than 100,000 patients, and his ads were full of testimonials—potentially false—from patients who claimed Fryer had cured them of cancer. One story was about a woman who had been cured of a cancer on her face: "We tried everything that we could hear of, both far and near, to cure this formidable enemy of the human race," her husband allegedly wrote, "but all to no purpose, until she took one package of Dr. W. K. F. Fryer's Concentrated Prescription of Vegetable Medicines, which course of treatment has cured her."

DOCTOR FRYER,

THE INDIAN DOCTOR,

IS a regular graduate of Nature's wide Botanic Garden and Common Sense Medical College, and has made the study of Herbs his profession for thirty years; and daily cures more patients than any other physician in New Orleans.

Fryer also offered a $25,000 reward to any physician who could "cure any of the following named diseases, quicker and with more safety, than I can." The list included yellow fever, consumption (tuberculosis), rheumatism, cholera, cancer, and venereal diseases, as well as "wind in the stomach," "chronic female weaknesses," "cold hands and feet," and gunshot wounds. Fryer also advertised a painless cure for stammering and stuttering, and he warned patients against "impudent quacks."

Fryer practiced in New Orleans until at least 1857, and in July 1858 he offered his traveling services to the residents of Jackson, Mississippi. After that the newspaper record is silent. Over the years, states increasingly regulated the medical profession, and it's possible that he was put out of business.

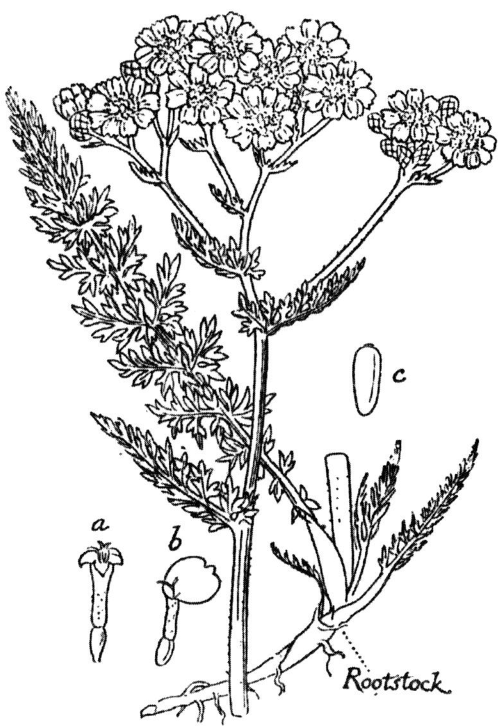

Fig. 87.—Yarrow or Milfoil (*Achillea Millefolium*)
a, Disk floret. *b*, Ray floret. *c*, Seed.

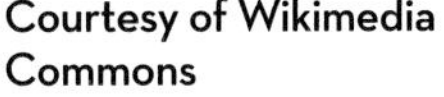
Courtesy of Wikimedia Commons

The *Governor Morton* steamboat. Courtesy of the Indiana Historical Society

The Farce of the Robert Hanna

When state officials chose the Fall Creek Settlement—later Indianapolis—as the site for the new state capital, they believed that the White River was navigable. The city would soon be a bustling riverport, they thought, with an easy connection to the Ohio River. But the river was too shallow, too clogged with debris, and too full of hidden sandbars to be of any use. Indianapolis was surrounded by unbroken wilderness, with no easy way in or out.

The people's hopes were revived on April 11, 1831, when a Captain Robert Hanna arrived in Indianapolis on a small steamship named after himself. He had a contract to build part of the National Road, and he planned to use the ship to transport stone and timber. The boat's arrival was a thrilling moment for early Indianapolis. The White River was navigable after all! Crowds gathered to see the miracle boat, which received an artillery salute from the local militia. Hanna and his crew were wined and dined, and a public meeting was held urging officials to survey the waterway and invest in port infrastructure.

The next day, April 12, the *Robert Hanna* offered short rides upriver. All went well until the last trip of the day, when overhanging branches knocked down the pilot house and chimneys. Some passengers were so frightened that they jumped overboard. But the damage was nothing that couldn't be fixed.

The day after that, April 13, the boat headed downriver, but it soon ran aground on a sandbar. It stayed stuck for six weeks. When the water finally rose, the *Robert Hanna* left and was never seen in Indianapolis again. It was time to accept the city's landlocked fate. As one historian remarked, "No power less than Omnipotence can do anything with so unpromising a case as White River."

Another Boat, Another Disaster

The White River is bad luck for boats. In July 1865, the steamboat *Governor Morton* was launched in Indianapolis to offer short cruises. In the boat's most profitable journey, it got stuck on a sandbar, and the crew served up $168 in drinks. In July 1866 it ran aground and was damaged, and in August it sank, just over a year after its maiden voyage.

The Curse of the Governor's Mansion

When Alexander Ralston laid out the plat for Indianapolis, he placed the governor's residence at the center of Monument Circle, where the Soldiers and Sailors Monument now stands. The house was built, but it was impossible to live in. It had no kitchen, for example, and no governor's wife wanted everyone to see her laundry hanging out to dry. So, no governor ever lived there, and it was eventually torn down. But amazingly, the second governor's mansion was an even worse disaster. That house had a knack for killing its residents.

Governor Oliver P. Morton
Courtesy of the Library of Congress

In 1839, the legislature bought the grandest house in the city for use as an executive mansion. Dr. John H. Sanders had built the two-story brick house, on the northwest corner of Illinois and Market, only a few years earlier. But "the governors all suffered there," one historian wrote. Gov. Samuel Bigger there contracted the illness that killed him shortly after leaving office. Gov. James Whitcomb's wife died in the house, and Gov. Joseph Wright lost *two* wives while living there. Gov. Ashbel Willard's family was sick for his entire gubernatorial term. When Gov. Oliver P. Morton moved into the house in 1861, his family got "so severely and unremittingly" sick that he moved everyone into a hotel until he could purchase a home of his own. He must have heard the stories.

The issue, wrote historian W. R. Holloway, was that the house sat "so far below the line of drainage, that in rainy weather it was surrounded by quite a pond of water, which kept the walls damp, molded the paper, spoiled provisions, and created constant sickness." Perhaps the issue was toxic mold. In 1865, the legislature ordered the property to be sold, and the state was without an official governor's residence until 1919.

A Ghostly Mystery

For a while, the first governor's mansion—the one on Monument Circle—was rumored to be haunted. But a group of brave boys investigated, and they discovered that the strange sound emanating from the building was just a turkey trapped in the cellar.

The first governor's residence on Monument Circle

The Irvington School War

Irvington, the first suburb of Indianapolis, was known for its tranquility and community spirit. But the Irvington School War of 1877, "the wildest excitement that ever developed," changed the neighborhood forever.

The teacher for the 1876-77 school year had been Lydia R. Putnam, and the school board renewed her contract for the following year. But then two of the three board members resigned, and they were replaced by men who opposed Putnam. The new board—Sylvester Johnson, James A. Krumrine, and William H. H. Shank—ignored Putnam's contract and hired a male teacher instead.

Controversy brewed all summer, with Irvington residents writing "spicy" letters to the editor and circulating petitions. The children of Irvington were baffled. Putnam was known as a dedicated and thorough teacher, though perhaps a bit too strict.

"To me she seemed the embodiment of all the virtues and proprieties, as well as the very wisest person of my acquaintance," one student recalled.

Putnam was not easily deterred. On the first day of school, she marched into the building, ducked under the outstretched arm of Krumrine, and took her seat at her desk. When the school board ordered her to leave, she stated "that she would do so only by due process of law."

The three men then grabbed Putnam and dragged her through a classroom full of dismayed young witnesses. Johnson and Krumrine each took an arm, with Shank "boosting with his knee" from behind. They removed her from the building and locked the front door, but Putnam ran to the back door, came inside, and again sat at her desk. They removed her again. This time she clung to a large staple in the wall until her fingers bled, but she eventually lost her grip.

Putnam was far from beaten, however. She had the board members arrested for assault and battery, and they were found guilty and fined $15 each. She then brought a civil suit against the school board, and she was awarded her promised salary of $800. Putnam did not teach in Irvington again, however, and the event deeply divided the community. "As with all wars, its aftermath was quite as painful and regrettable as the actual fray," wrote one of the students, Grace Julian Clarke, in the *Indianapolis Star*. "Old friends and neighbors no longer spoke to one another, [and] enmities were engendered that men carried to their graves."

Courtesy of the Indiana State Library

The Poster Family for Eugenics

An Indianapolis family was prominently featured at the 1933 World's Fair in Chicago—but not in a good way. A "scientific" eugenics display described the Ishmael family as feeble-minded criminals and beggars that "lacked the basic qualities of intelligence and character" to be successful. Because these qualities were seen as hereditary, the display suggested, the best solution was forced sterilization.

For decades, the Ishmael family was "synonymous with the undeserving poor in the United States" who were unworthy of charitable assistance. They were "discovered" in 1877 by pastor Oscar McCulloch as he ministered to the poor. "I visited a case of extreme destitution," he wrote. "There were gathered in one room, without fire, an old blind woman, a man, his wife and one child, his sister, and two children. A half-bed was all the furnishing." McColloch spent the next decade researching the Ishmael family. He blamed them for committing most of the city's crimes and for using a disproportionate amount of township poverty relief. He frequently compared them to animals. The Ishmael family did exist, and they were desperately poor. But McCulloch claimed they were at the center of 250 interconnected families, encompassing thousands of people who were hereditarily predisposed to poverty. He called them the "tribe of Ishmael," and wrote, "They underrun society like devil-grass."

In the 1920s, eugenicist Arthur Estabrook did a follow-up study on the family. Then, although the Ishmaels were white and had immigrated, most likely from Wales, way back in the 1700s, they somehow became a symbol of the dangers of unrestricted immigration from the East. Estabrook's study was even discussed in Congress during debates about the Immigration Act of 1924, which prohibited almost all immigration from Asia.

After the World's Fair in 1933, the eugenics movement became increasingly controversial, and the Ishmaels were forgotten. Then, in the 1970s, they were "rediscovered" and radically reinvented by Hugo Prosper Leaming. Despite all evidence to the contrary, he claimed Benjamin Ishmael was a Muslim of African descent, and that the Ishmaels were actually a multi-racial Islamic family with a distinct culture. He was wrong, however, and his research was soon discredited. The Ishmaels were—had always been—just an ordinary family in Indianapolis.

Oscar McCulloch
Courtesy of the Indiana State Library

Courtesy of the Smithsonian

The Death of Leonidas Grover

The *Indianapolis Journal* reported a shocking story on January 16, 1879. While sleeping in his bed, Leonidas Grover of Fountain County had been killed by a 20-pound meteorite. It had come through the roof, crushed the bed, and lodged itself five feet below the floor of his bedroom. His daughter had discovered the incident the next morning when she went to call Grover to breakfast.

The story caused a sensation. It was reprinted in other newspapers and was even mentioned in a scientific study. The state geologist, Edward Travers Cox, sent John J. Palmer to Fountain County to investigate further. Palmer soon returned with the meteorite, a photo of Leonidas Grover, and a map of the house's layout, all of which he put on display at a downtown drugstore.

The only problem: the story wasn't true. As a prank, a staff member at the *Journal* had slipped the fake story into a pile of other articles. When Palmer had arrived in Fountain County, he had discovered the hoax and decided to keep it going. His "meteorite" was just a painted rock.

The *Journal* had to admit its mistake. "We take it back in its totality," wrote editor George C. Harding. "The death was not a phenomenal one. The aerolite did not come hurtling from the infinite depths of space. It did not tear a ragged opening through the roof of Mr. Grover's house, nor did it crash through his breast . . . He didn't die. He didn't get hurt. He didn't even get frightened. He wasn't there. He isn't anywhere."

The chagrined editor added, "If Mr. Leonidas Grover ever should come into existence and get killed by an aerolite, he will have to get someone else to write his obituary."

April Fools

On April 1, 1929, police headquarters in Indianapolis was inundated with calls asking for a Mr. Ketcham. The exasperated switchboard operator finally started replying, "All policemen catch 'em. Which one do you want?" The pranksters also called the city animal shelter, asking for Mr. Shepherd and Mr. Beagle.

Cocktail Charlie

Vice President Charles W. Fairbanks of Indianapolis was known for abstaining from alcohol. His teetotaling ways had even earned him the nickname "Buttermilk Charlie." Nevertheless, it was alcohol that destroyed his political career.

On Memorial Day in May 1907, President Theodore Roosevelt came to Indianapolis to dedicate a statue of Spanish-American War hero Henry W. Lawton. As part of his visit, he attended a luncheon at Fairbanks's home on Meridian Street, alongside local politicians, writers, and business leaders. James Whitcomb Riley was on the guest list, as was future diplomat Meredith Nicholson. Fairbanks's wife prepared a menu of planked whitefish and broiled spring chicken. At the last minute, a friend of hers realized that they'd forgotten the cocktails. She telephoned the Columbia Club, which delivered 40 Manhattans just in time for the meal. Some newspapers reported that wine was also served. Alcohol was legal at that time; it would be another decade before the state went dry. Nevertheless, the cocktails caused quite a scandal. Soon

Guests at the infamous luncheon
Courtesy of the Indiana Historical Society

Fairbanks had been re-christened as "Champagne Charlie" and more commonly "Cocktail Charlie."

"Temperance people [are] agitated and newspapers [are] having lots of fun over cocktails served by Vice President Fairbanks," one newspaper reported. "They say the VP cannot be 'Buttermilk Charlie' to the temperance people and 'Champagne Charlie' to the boys and get away with it." In other words, Fairbanks was branded a hypocrite.

President Roosevelt stayed silent on the issue. "If it pleases the Indianapolis teetotalers to jump on him because they have been told of certain occurrences that may or may not have taken place, the president will certainly not add to nor spoil their satisfaction by replying," stated a White House official. "He . . . will not get all heated up over such a small matter."

The following year, Fairbanks was passed over as the Republican nominee for president, in part because of the scandal. He made another run for the vice presidency in 1916, on the ticket with Charles Evans Hughes, but was unsuccessful. He died two years later and is buried at Crown Hill Cemetery.

The Marketing Genius of Carl Fisher

Courtesy of the Library of Congress

One day in 1908, Indianapolis auto dealer Carl Fisher attracted national attention with a promotional stunt. He strapped a new Stoddard-Dayton automobile to an enormous hot-air balloon, and he rode in the car as it floated over the city. When the balloon landed, Fisher unhooked the car from the balloon and drove it away.

Actually, Fisher drove an identical version of the car. The one attached to the balloon had been stripped of its engine to reduce its weight. But nobody knew that at the time. For Indianapolis it was yet another example of Fisher's daring and his incredible marketing skills.

Fisher got his start in business by selling candy and newspapers on trains. At the age of 17, he opened a bicycle repair shop on Pennsylvania Street with his brothers, capitalizing on the cycling craze of the 1890s. Soon he started selling bicycles as well as repairing them.

To promote the business, Fisher constructed a 20-foot bicycle and rode it around town, waving at office workers on the second floors of the buildings he passed. He also strung a tightrope between two buildings on Washington Street and rode across on a bicycle. Once, he released hundreds of balloons with attached tags, some of which entitled the finder to a free bicycle. And once he threw a bicycle off the city's tallest building, promising a new bicycle to whoever returned the damaged one to his shop.

When the cycling trend started to wane, Fisher transformed the shop into an auto dealership—possibly the first in the nation. To prove one car's durability, he pushed it off a building roof and then drove it away. He also staged road races with rival dealers. But the stunt with the hot-air balloon earned by far the most attention: 5,000 people gathered to watch its ascent.

Fisher's promotional prowess made him a rich man. He went on to co-found the Indianapolis Motor Speedway and the Indianapolis 500, and later he developed the resort community of Miami Beach.

Fisher Fools the Police Force

The police department tried to stop Fisher from throwing a bicycle off the city's tallest building, given that the stunt was potentially dangerous. They surrounded the building that morning to prevent him from accessing it—not realizing that he'd gone inside the night before. Fisher had slept on the roof, and he dropped the bicycle as planned.

The Indy Stunts of Harry Houdini

Harry Houdini performed in Indianapolis at least four times during his celebrated vaudeville career, escaping from straightjackets, handcuffs, shackles, and many other constraints. Each time, Houdini customized his performance by incorporating local people and companies into his act—sometimes to their delight, and sometimes to their eternal shame.

Houdini's first visit to Indianapolis was probably in 1907–08, when the New Grand Theater featured "the world-famous handcuff king and sensational prison breaker." The act must have been a hit, because the engagement was extended for a second week.

Houdini returned to the city in 1911. This time he generated publicity by walking into police headquarters and asking Detective Capt. William Holtz to lock him up. Holtz chose five pairs of handcuffs from different manufacturers, put them on Houdini personally, and

Courtesy of the Library of Congress

retained the keys. The escape took all of six minutes, but Houdini called it "one of the severest tests I have ever undergone."

In both 1911 and his next visit in 1915, Houdini accepted a challenge from the Indianapolis Brewing Company to escape from a tank of its Lieber's Special Brew. He succeeded both times. And in 1925, he escaped from a container that had been specially constructed for the purpose by the L. S. Ayres shipping department.

But not everyone enjoyed being part of the act. Houdini was known for debunking spiritualists who claimed to communicate with the dead, and in 1925 he publicly accused a local minister, Charles H. Gunsolus, and presented evidence gathered by private detectives. Gunsolus was unable to refute the charges, and the crowd turned against him. He was ruined.

Houdini generated his biggest Indianapolis headlines on that visit in 1925, when B. F. Keith's advertised his "triumphant return after ten years' absence." On April 2, he attracted a crowd of thousands by escaping from a straightjacket while suspended upside down by his ankles over Washington Street. The escape, which took three minutes, was one of the last times Houdini performed that particular trick. He died of a ruptured appendix the following year, at age 52, on Halloween.

The Search for a Snake Hostess

An unusual "help wanted" article ran in the *Indianapolis Star* on June 30, 1924. The Shriners of the Murat Temple were planning a birthday party for King, a South American boa constrictor, and they were hiring a hostess for the party. All the hostess had to do was sit in the snake pit during the party—along with seven 200-pound pythons and boa constrictors.

"The hostess should see to it that the snakes behave themselves, so they won't fight each other," said organizer Robert L. Elder. "Any charming woman should have no trouble making them behave."

Courtesy of Pixabay and Ambquinn

Like any good hostess, this one would also have to feed her guests. The menu consisted of live white rats, guinea pigs, toads, chickens, and rabbits. The good news, Elder said, was that the snakes were not venomous. "The snakes kill their prey by squeezing," he said, "and the hostess may get a hug or two, but attendants will see that the hugs will not be too ardent." The payment was "a purse of gold" of unspecified value.

The next day the *Indianapolis Star* announced that five women had applied for the position. Four of the applicants had no prior experience with snakes, but one, a Mrs. Oakie Scott, had a collection of house pets "comprising every reptile native to Indiana." If she was selected, she planned to bring her snakes along as guests.

By the next day, the number of applicants had climbed to 11, and the position went to a Georgia Rudd of North East Street. The *Star* read, "Miss Rudd has had some experience with snakes, she asserts, but has never handled a 16-foot monster python in a den of numerous 200-pound reptiles."

The lack of experience didn't stop Rudd. She fulfilled her hostess duties "to the awe and admiration of hundreds of persons who visited the Shrine show last night," the *Star* reported a few days later.

"I do not think I should be classed as a heroine because of this stunt tonight," Rudd said. "Almost any other woman could have done the same if she had made up her mind to it." She also stated that she might pursue a career in snake handling.

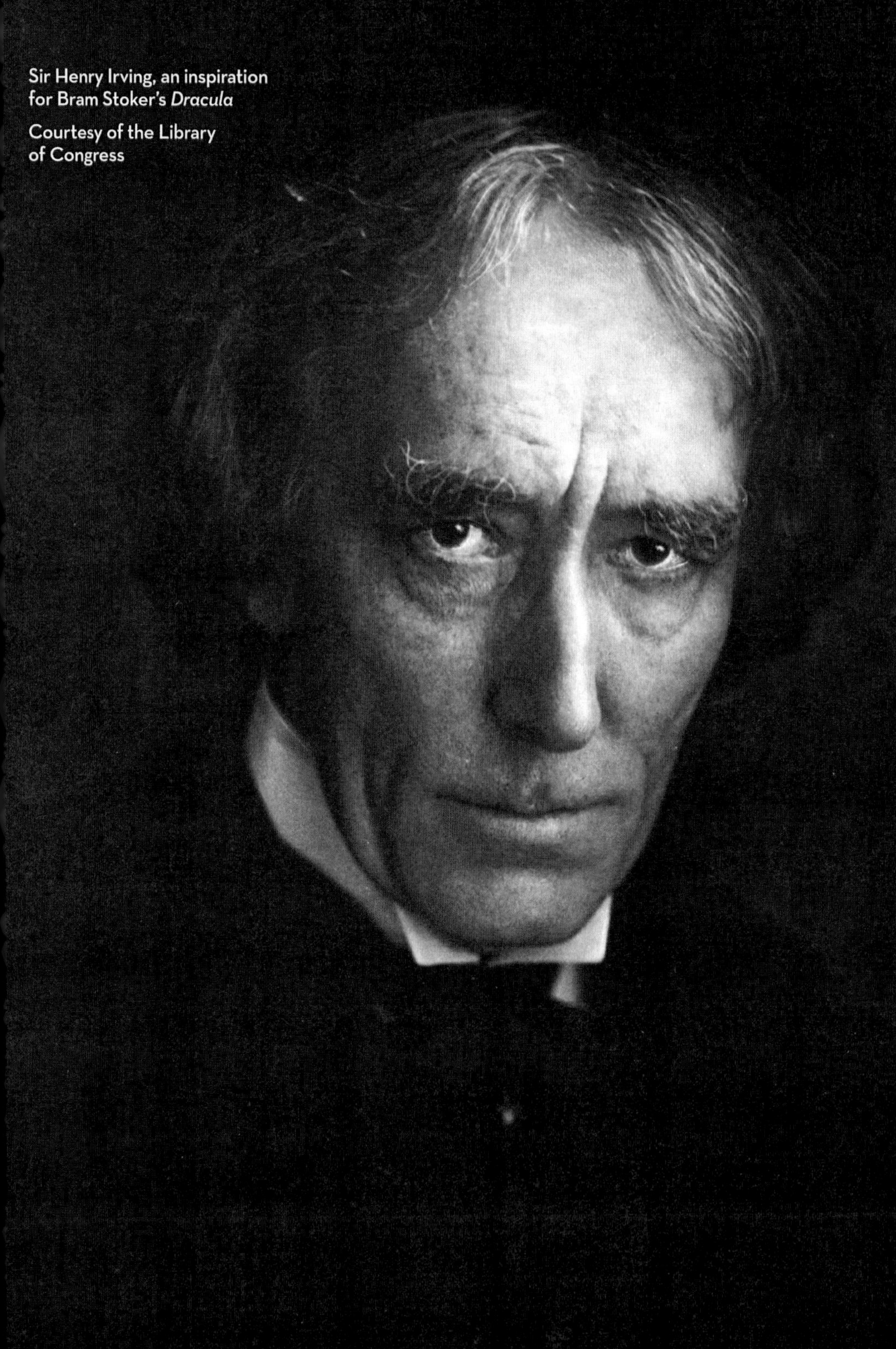

Sir Henry Irving, an inspiration for Bram Stoker's *Dracula*

Courtesy of the Library of Congress

Chapter Six

Surprising Connections

Before Bram Stoker wrote the famous *Dracula*, he was stirring up controversy in Indianapolis. Before Harriet Beecher Stowe wrote *Uncle Tom's Cabin*, she visited here and met a formerly enslaved man nicknamed Uncle Tom. Before John Wilkes Booth assassinated President Abraham Lincoln, the celebrated actor performed here—receiving a few scathing reviews along the way. And before Jim Jones founded his deadly cult, he sold monkeys door to door in Indianapolis.

This chapter is about the city's unexpected and unknown links with national news and cultural touchstones. One Indianapolis native wrote every single episode of *I Love Lucy*, for example. Both John Muir and Thomas Edison lived here briefly, and those visits were life-changing for both men. It turns out, the Circle City has been at the center of a surprising number of historic events.

Courtesy of the Library of Congress

John Muir's Indy Ordeal

Before John Muir became a beloved nature writer and the "father of the conservation movement," he was a terrified and confused young man in Indianapolis. He started his life in Scotland, then immigrated to Wisconsin, where his family built a farm in the wilderness. Although he had a difficult childhood—his father forbade music and any books other than the Bible—he was irrepressibly curious about the world around him. As a teenager, Muir started to tinker, and soon he was building all sorts of mechanical devices. He knew he had talent as an inventor. But what he really wanted was to live life outdoors as a wandering botanist.

In 1866, after a few years of college and a few odd jobs, Muir came to the boom town of Indianapolis in search of work. He took a position in a factory that churned out farming implements, and he was quickly promoted. "Circumstances over which I have no control almost compel me to abandon the profession of my choice, and take up the business of an inventor," he wrote to his sister.

Then came the accident that changed his life. On March 6, 1867, he was repairing a piece of equipment when a file "flew out of his hand and pierced his right eye," one biographer wrote. He lost the vision in his right eye, and his left eye went dark, too, in sympathy. "I could gladly have died on the spot," Muir wrote to a friend, "because I did not feel that I could . . . look at any flower again."

Muir lay for days in a darkened bedroom, not knowing whether his vision would return. He had never been more miserable. But he slowly regained his eyesight, and the recovery period gave him time to think deeply about his next move. Now he knew that a life amongst machinery was not for him. His path was outdoors.

Muir later became the first president of the Sierra Club, and he lobbied fiercely for the creation of national parks to preserve America's wild places. Thanks to Muir's influence, President Theodore Roosevelt established five national parks during his presidency and classified several other wild sites as national monuments.

Thomas Edison's Light Bulb Moment

In a typical biography of Thomas Edison, his time in Indianapolis—where he turned 18—merits only two or three pages. The future inventor of the phonograph, light bulb, and alkaline battery lived here for only a few months, but his time here inspired one of his most celebrated inventions.

During the Civil War, skilled telegraph operators were in high demand. Edison floated from city to city, sure of finding a job wherever he landed. In the fall of 1864, Edison wandered into Indianapolis, where he took a job for the Western Union Telegraph Company, based at the Union Depot, for $75 per month.

One of Edison's frustrations was the speed at which news reports were sent over the wire: up to 40 words per minute. Transcribing these reports for the local newspapers often meant paraphrasing or leaving sections out, just to keep up. So, Edison invented a "repeater," using two embossing Morse registers, to record the incoming reports on a paper cylinder. Edison could then replay the messages at a slower speed for easier transcription, in handwriting that was easier to read.

What happened next is uncertain. One biographer stated that "the newspapers were more anxious for the news than they were for fine penmanship," and they complained about the delayed reports. Another claimed that Edison's colleagues objected because they were embarrassed by the high quality of his transcriptions. Either way, Edison's boss investigated, discovered the device, and banned its use. Probably because of this incident, Edison left Indianapolis in February 1865.

But Edison never forgot that early invention. "This instrument, many years afterward, was applied by me for transferring messages from one wire to any other wire simultaneously, or after any interval of time," he later said. "It was this instrument which gave me the idea of the phonograph."

Courtesy of the Library of Congress

Actor Turned Assassin

Before John Wilkes Booth became a killer, he was a celebrated actor best known for his roles in Shakespeare plays. He performed at theaters across the country, among them the Metropolitan Theatre in Indianapolis.

Booth first visited Indianapolis in December 1861. On Christmas Day, he played the title role in *Richard III*. The *Indianapolis Daily Sentinel* stated, "How so young a man could so perfectly personate the old, crooked-backed tyrant surpassed all our conceptions of theatricals before." The *Sentinel* was equally impressed the following day, when Booth played the title role in *Othello*; the newspaper wrote, "We anticipated a good performance but were not prepared for so great an outburst of genius." He performed in several other plays later that week, including *Hamlet* and *Macbeth*.

In November 1862, Booth was back at the Metropolitan, performing in *Othello*, *Macbeth*, *Hamlet*, and several other plays. He received good reviews overall, but the *Indianapolis Daily Journal* called his portrayal of Othello a "failure." The reviewer wrote, "We don't admire Mr. Booth, and by what art he became a 'star' is more than our astronomy can explain." Other reviews that week, however, called his work "splendid" and "a masterpiece of acting."

A few weeks later, in January 1863, Booth returned to Indianapolis. He opened with *Hamlet*, and the *Sentinel* wrote, "Mr. Booth is indeed a great actor, and appears to have a true conception of the character of the melancholy prince." The following day Booth again portrayed the title character in *Othello*, and local newspapers gave the performance mixed reviews. But the *Enquirer* noted, "An opportunity of seeing his equal . . . is exceedingly rare in this neck of the woods." He performed at the Metropolitan for four more evenings, ending with his popular portrayal of Richard III.

Courtesy of the Library of Congress

Later that year, Booth made his first appearance at the new Ford's Theatre in Washington, DC. During a two-week engagement, he performed in *Richard III*, *The Merchant of Venice*, *Hamlet*, *Romeo and Juliet*, and several other plays. But when he visited the same theater on April 14, 1865, it was to assassinate President Abraham Lincoln.

The Inspiration for *Uncle Tom's Cabin*

When Indy's Second Presbyterian Church hired minister Henry Ward Beecher in 1839, he was only two years out of seminary. Eventually he would gain a national reputation as an abolitionist, speaker, and social reformer, but in Indianapolis he led a quieter life: preaching, tending his garden, and welcoming visits from his sister, Harriet Beecher Stowe.

Stowe, of course, later authored *Uncle Tom's Cabin*, one of the best-selling novels of the 19th century. She always maintained that Uncle Tom was a composite character, but Indianapolis thought differently. During her time in the city, Stowe frequently met with Tom Magruder, known as Uncle Tom, who had formerly been enslaved in Virginia. He lived in a cabin at the northeast corner of Noble and Market. Stowe took copious notes during their conversations, and then she populated her fictional world with characters named after members of Magruder's family. When Magruder died in 1857, the *Indianapolis Journal* noted "the probability that he gave the name and the leading features of the character to Mrs. Stowe's celebrated hero."

To be fair, Magruder wasn't the only man to be identified as the "real" Uncle Tom. Another possibility was Josiah Henson,

Courtesy of the Library of Congress

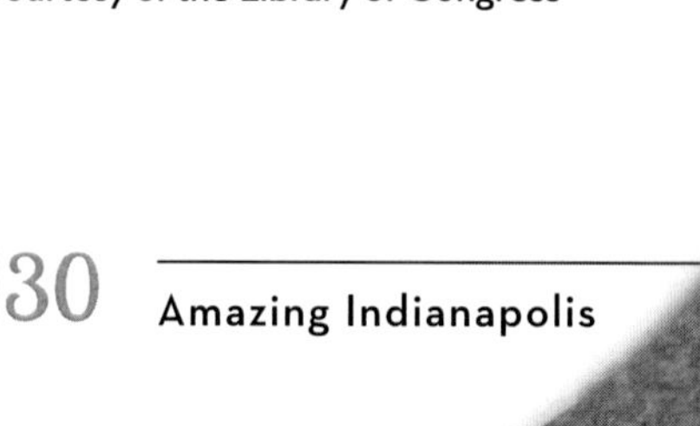

Courtesy of the Boston Public Library

who told his story in *The Life of Josiah Henson, Formerly a Slave, Now an Inhabitant of Canada*, which was published in 1849. Henson met Stowe later that year, and he wrote that she "was deeply interested in the story of my life and misfortunes." Another possibility was John Andrew Jackson, who stayed at Stowe's home while escaping slavery in the Carolinas. But, as this is a book about Indianapolis, let's err on the side of Magruder.

Fanny Van de Grift

Indianapolis had another 19th-century literary connection in resident Fanny Van de Grift. She was traveling in France in the 1870s when she met the writer Robert Louis Stevenson, and they married in 1880. Stevenson later wrote such classics as *Treasure Island, A Child's Garden of Verse,* and *The Strange Case of Dr. Jekyll and Mr. Hyde.*

The *Dracula* Connection

Bram Stoker drew on a number of influences for his famous *Dracula*, including historical figures, folklore, gothic novels . . . and just maybe his experiences on the streets of Indianapolis.

Stoker's day job was managing the career of actor Sir Henry Irving, who appeared in costume on some of *Dracula*'s book covers. Irving's work brought him to Indianapolis four times between 1884 and 1904, and Stoker was with him each time. But it's surprising that either returned to town after the first visit, during which Irving and Ellen Terry presented Shakespeare's *The Merchant of Venice* and portions of Boucicault's *Louis XI*. Soon after that visit, Stoker caused controversy locally when he was quoted in the *New York Herald* calling Indianapolis "a one-horsey town." His boss then said, "All I have to say is that Indianapolis theater may become a very good place of amusement, but the town has too many fat ladies." Stoker added, "And dog shows."

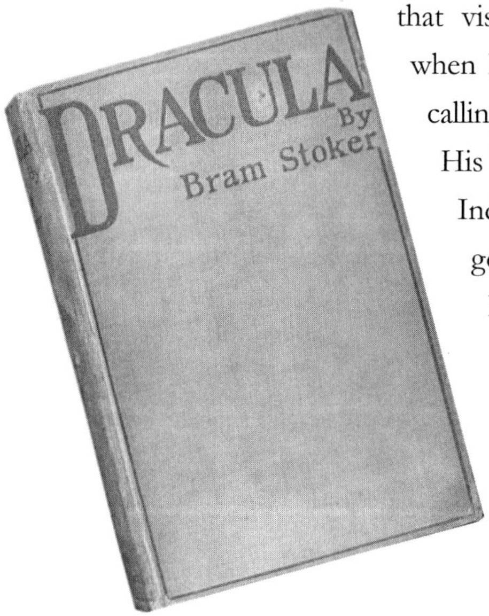

Despite the insults, the duo returned to Indianapolis in 1896, 1902, and 1904. In 1896, Irving and Terry performed at English's

Opera House as Shylock and Portia in *The Merchant of Venice*, and as Arthur and Guinivere in the J. Comyns Carr play *King Arthur*. During that visit, the *Indianapolis Journal* described Stoker as "tall, broad-shouldered, faultlessly dressed, with an eye that takes in a hundred different objects at a glance, busy yet imperturbable, peremptory yet urbane." The newspaper credited Stoker with "a very large share of Irving's good fortune during the last decade and a half." Oddly, the newspaper also praised Stoker's tact and said he was well-suited for diplomacy. Perhaps by then Stoker's insults had been forgotten.

An Insult from Oscar Wilde

Another Irish writer, Oscar Wilde, was at English's Opera House on February 22, 1882, to deliver a lecture titled "The English Renaissance." The *Indianapolis News* wrote derisively, "He is not disseminating news about art, but gathering dollars." After the lecture, Wilde attended a party hosted by the governor, whom he thanked for "this opportunity of observing the peasantry of Indiana."

Courtesy of the Library of Congress

Courtesy of the Library of Congress

A Visit from a Chinese Prince

In 1904, Prince Pu Lun—heir apparent to the throne of China—came to the United States for the Louisiana Purchase Exposition in St. Louis. But along the way he wanted to experience a typical American city. He chose Indianapolis.

"Prince Pu Lun is much impressed with Indianapolis from what he has heard of it," said visit organizer William Fortune. "He has chosen this city as the one in which he wants to study American ideas—commercially, industrially, and socially."

The prince arrived by train on May 18 and was whisked through the large crowds to an official reception at the Statehouse. Local newspapers breathlessly reported the prince's every move, describing his clothes, the decor of his hotel suite, and even the pattern of china used at the luxurious Claypool Hotel, where he stayed.

During his visit to the Circle City, the prince visited factories, schools, prisons, and hospitals. He also went to the top of the Soldiers & Sailors Monument, attended a performance at English's Opera House, and went on a day trip to Purdue University. He thrilled a local businessman, who was a Chinese immigrant, by consenting to dine at his restaurant. He also went to a baseball game, saw a dog and pony show, and attended a demonstration of x-ray technology. He made a point of visiting Fairview Park to see the famous diving horses there, and he had his palm read by "palmist to the stars" Nellie Simmons Meier.

There were a few diplomatic snafus along the way, however. Local ministers protested that the prince's itinerary didn't include a church service. Members of the Local Council of Women were infuriated when the prince arrived more than an hour late for a large reception; he had insisted on taking a nap beforehand. And after attending an exhibition of girls' athletics, he mentioned how much he admired their big feet.

The prince—who never did become emperor of China—left the city on May 27. "Indianapolis has somewhat cooled down from the excitement incident to the visit of a real live prince," the *Muncie Herald* reported. "It seems as though the female portion . . . of the capital city was in a wild frenzy."

Jim Jones, Monkey Salesman

Long before he became a notorious cult leader, and long before his followers died in the largest mass suicide in history, Jim Jones was a seemingly harmless minister in Indianapolis. And while he was here, he raised money for his church by selling monkeys door to door. They cost $29 apiece.

Jones began importing six-month-old spider monkeys and gibbons from India sometime in 1953. In addition to selling them, he awarded them as prizes to church members who brought the most new members into the congregation. But Jones made the front page on April 10, 1954, by refusing a shipment of dead and dying monkeys, leaving them in the care of a bewildered customs agent.

From a shipment of seven monkeys, only three had survived the journey to Indianapolis. They had received no food or water en route from New York, a trip that took six days because of an airline snafu. The quick-thinking customs agent revived the surviving three with mashed bananas and generous helpings of confiscated German apple-jack brandy. A string of state agencies then refused to take responsibility for the monkeys, and eventually they were assigned to an animal shelter for the weekend, with plans to sell them at auction the following Monday "after they have fattened—and sobered—up."

Two of the monkeys—one did not survive the weekend—were indeed put on the auction block, and they sold as a package deal for $51 to an A. E. Stipp of Maywood. He said he hoped the monkeys would draw crowds to the railroad salvage business he planned to open later that week.

The monkeys Jones had previously sold rarely fared much better. One was gunned down by police in June after escaping his home. And

Courtesy of Pixabay and Akiroz Brost

the *Indianapolis Star* classifieds that year were full of advertisements for spider monkeys and gibbons, who were no longer wanted once the novelty wore off.

Shortridge High School
Courtesy of the Indianapolis Public Library

The Woman Behind *I Love Lucy*

Because Lucille Ball was such a gifted comedian, everyone assumed her slapstick antics on *I Love Lucy* were improvised. But, in fact, those moments were carefully scripted by the writing team of Bob Carroll and "girl writer" Madelyn Pugh Davis, who was born and raised in Indianapolis.

"I used to try [the stunts] first because we wanted to see if it was physically possible for a woman to do, and we also wanted to make sure Lucy wouldn't get hurt," Davis wrote in her memoir. She learned how to dip chocolate candy, walk on stilts, and carry eggs around in her bra. She practiced pitching Vitameatavegamin. She even tried riding a unicycle, but she crashed—so that stunt never made it onto the show.

Growing up on Central Avenue in Indianapolis, Davis knew she wanted to be a writer. She penned her first play at the age of 10, and soon her mother bought her a second-hand typewriter. She attended Shortridge High School, where she worked on the *Daily Echo*, and Indiana University, where she majored in journalism and worked on the *Indiana Daily Student.*

The US entered World War II while Davis was in college. "I wouldn't have had any career at all if it weren't for World War II," Davis wrote. In her first job, as a writer for Indianapolis radio station WIRE, she replaced a man who had joined the Navy.

After a year at WIRE, Davis moved to Los Angeles. She worked briefly for the NBC Radio Network before moving to CBS, where she met Carroll. After a few years, they joined the writing team for the radio show *My Favorite Husband*, starring Lucille Ball. That show evolved into TV's groundbreaking *I Love Lucy*. Carroll and Davis wrote every episode of that show, and they also worked with Ball on later shows such as *The Lucy Show* and *Here's Lucy*.

In all, Carroll and Davis worked together for half a century, writing roughly 300 radio shows and 400 TV shows. They also had 250 producer credits and wrote several movies, including Ball's *Yours, Mine, and Ours*. After a long and trailblazing career, Davis died in 2011 at the age of 90.

The interior of Union Station, 1888

Chapter Seven

The First, Oldest, and Largest

Indianapolis can lay claim to many superlatives. It has the largest children's museum in the world, and the Indianapolis Motor Speedway is the world's largest venue for spectator sports. Our Union Depot (later Union Station) was the first such unified train station in the nation. And the city used to have the oldest continuously operating community theater in the nation . . . but that's a whole story in itself.

This chapter is all about the biggest and the best. It includes Crown Hill Cemetery, one of the largest non-governmental cemeteries in the nation. And it includes the International Orangutan Center at the Indianapolis Zoo, one of the largest exhibits of its kind in the world. Hoosiers may be humble, but this chapter proves that Indianapolis has plenty to brag about.

Union Depot and Union Station

Indianapolis was the "crossroads of America" long before interstates crisscrossed and surrounded the city. It earned that title in the 1800s, when the city became a hub for Midwest railroad traffic. And it accomplished that, in part, by building the first "union" train station in the nation.

The first train arrived in Indianapolis on October 1, 1847, and soon several more railroads were being planned. In most cities, each railroad company had its own depot, and passengers might have to rush across the city from one depot to another to catch their next train. Very early, city leaders realized that passengers would benefit from a central depot that accommodated every passenger train in the city.

The Union Depot opened in September 1853 with five indoor tracks for passenger trains. "It was just a great barn, 425 feet long by 200 feet wide," wrote historian John H. White. "[It was] a cheap commercial structure built for a purpose rather than a look." By 1870, the station was serving 11 railroad companies and about 75 trains per day—about 2 million passengers per year. "No equal convenience of a like character is found anywhere else in the country," wrote historian W. R. Holloway that year. "The ends of the earth, so to speak, are here brought into connection under one roof." But in 1883, a 15th railroad company requested access to the station, and city leaders had to acknowledge that the depot was too small.

Completed in 1888, the new Union Station had a three-story, barrel-vaulted waiting room that felt like a cathedral. There were separate waiting rooms for men and women, a barbershop, a dining room, and a lunch counter. At the dawn of the 20th century, the station was accommodating more than 150 passenger trains per day.

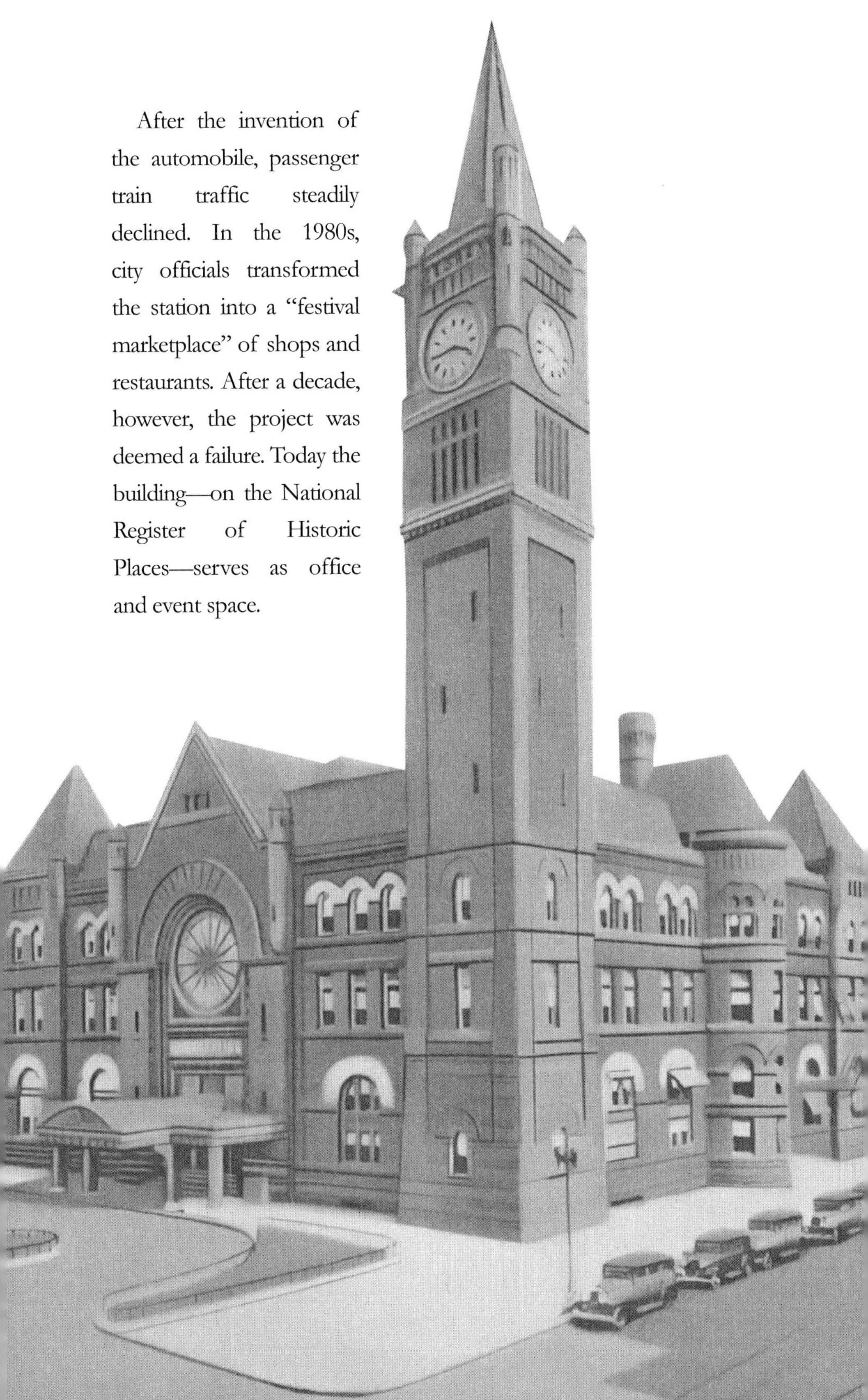

After the invention of the automobile, passenger train traffic steadily declined. In the 1980s, city officials transformed the station into a "festival marketplace" of shops and restaurants. After a decade, however, the project was deemed a failure. Today the building—on the National Register of Historic Places—serves as office and event space.

The theater on Alabama Street, c. 1930
Courtesy of the Bass Photo Co. Collection, Indiana Historical Society

The Booth Tarkington Civic Theatre

A tug-of-war erupted in 2009 between Indianapolis and its northern neighbor, Carmel. The latter had a new Center for the Performing Arts, and it offered the Civic Theatre of Indianapolis a 100-year lease to become one of its resident theater companies. As the oldest continuously operating community theater in the nation, Civic was an important part of the Indy arts scene. But the troupe needed a home, and it accepted the deal, moving north and becoming the Booth Tarkington Civic Theatre.

The Civic was founded in Indianapolis in 1914 as the Little Theatre Society of Indiana. It was part of a nationwide trend of renewed interest in community theater, in which the actors, directors, and backstage personnel were all amateur volunteers. The troupe made its debut on October 30, 1915, in the sculpture court at the Herron Art Institute. The scenery had been painted in a nearby barn and moved in hay wagons.

The sculpture garden had its limitations as a performance space, and in 1925-26 the Little Theatre Society built its own theater on Alabama Street. A few years later, the company changed its name to the Civic Theatre of Indianapolis. But by the 1960s attendance had declined. The board of directors judged the theater's location to be undesirable, and in 1973 they authorized the construction of a theater at the Indianapolis Museum of Art. Another solution was to restructure as a semi-professional theater company, with several paid staff members.

By 2004, the Indianapolis Museum of Art had its own ambitious construction plans, and it chose not to renew Civic's lease on the theater. As a temporary solution, the evicted troupe moved to the auditorium at Marian University. Meanwhile, it started the search for a new permanent home.

The offer from the Center for the Performing Arts was "by far the most beneficial proposal for Civic," said communications manager Marni Lemons. "We were not finding the level of support in Indianapolis that made it financially viable [to stay]."

Thus, the oldest community theater group in the nation settled down in Carmel instead of Indianapolis. Fortunately, most of its volunteers and patrons have been willing to make the trip north.

The Children's Museum

If you grow up in Indianapolis, it's easy to take the Children's Museum for granted. You play on the Reuben Wells steam engine, romp through Playscape, dig for bones in Dinosphere, go to planetarium shows, ride the historic carousel, explore ScienceWorks, and watch as the water clock marks the hour, never realizing that you are learning and playing at the largest children's museum in the world.

The beloved museum was founded in 1925 by Mary Stewart Carey, who was inspired by a similar museum in Brooklyn. The museum had several homes in its first few years, including a carriage house, a park shelter house, and the former Carey home on North Meridian Street. The first item donated to the museum's collection was a mounted porcupine fish; the first educational program was a Danish woman demonstrating the spinning wheel while her grandson translated. The museum moved to its present location in 1946, and the current building—a five-story structure centered on a spiral ramp—was constructed in the 1970s. A soaring Dale Chihuly sculpture, *Fireworks of Glass*, was added in 2006. And in 2018, the museum debuted the Sports Legends Experience, with indoor and outdoor galleries focused on fitness.

The museum is also home to more than 130,000 artifacts. These include cultural icons—for example, Barbie dolls and Batman toys—as well as scientific specimens. The list includes a meteorite, a genuine T. rex skeleton, and a taxidermied polar bear named Martimus.

Other galleries at the museum include "National Geographic Treasures of the Earth" and "The Power of Children," which celebrates Anne Frank, Ryan White, Ruby Bridges, and other young heroes. The

Courtesy of the Children's Museum of Indianapolis

"Take Me There" gallery highlights foreign countries such as Egypt, China, and Greece. And in the "Beyond Spaceship Earth" gallery, children can explore a re-creation of the International Space Station.

The museum now welcomes 1.2 million visitors each year, and it stays true to its stated mission: "to ignite joy, wonder, and curiosity."

Courtesy of Wikimedia Commons

The International Orangutan Center

The islands of Borneo and Sumatra are the only native habitat remaining for orangutans, which are among the most endangered species on the planet. But the Indianapolis Zoo is home to 11 of the great apes. The $26 million Simon Skjodt International Orangutan Center, which opened in 2014, is one of the largest exhibits of its kind.

"I can't think of another facility that rivals this one," said Rob Shumaker, vice president of conservation and life sciences for the zoo, in an *Indianapolis Star* article at the time. "This is truly an exceptional facility."

Every element of the exhibit was designed with the orangutans in mind. Orangutans are the largest arboreal animals on the planet, spending most of their time in the forest canopy. So, the exhibit incorporates a network of cables, platforms, and bridges from 45 to 80 feet above the ground to re-create that experience. A four-season atrium provides shelter in rough weather, and it enables zoo guests to see the orangutans up close.

The International Orangutan Center gives the animals choices about how and where to spend their time. Although orangutans have a complex social system, there are "oasis" spaces where they can choose to be alone. Researchers offer the apes daily computer-based cognitive tasks to create opportunities for learning and problem-solving, but the apes choose whether to participate.

Like humans, each orangutan has a distinct personality. Azy, the "gentle giant," is the peacekeeper of the group; he is intelligent, patient, and social. Katy is a bit flirty, and she loves using the computer for cognitive tasks. Basan, one of the youngest orangutans in the group, is cautious and shy, but he enjoys playing with water. The other residents are Charly, Lucy, Mila, Rocky, Nicky, Knobi, Sirih, and Max.

People of the Forest

The word orangutan comes from the Malay words *orang*, meaning "people," and *hutan*, meaning "of the forest." These "people of the forest" are not monkeys; they are great apes, as are chimpanzees, gorillas, bonobos, and humans. They have long lifespans (about 60 years) and very long arms—about 9 feet from fingertip to fingertip for an adult male orangutan.

Courtesy of the Library of Congress

Crown Hill Cemetery

The biographies of famous Indianapolis residents always seem to end with the same phrase: "buried at Crown Hill Cemetery." More than 200,000 people have been laid to rest at the cemetery since it opened in 1864, but there's still plenty of room: its acreage makes it the third largest non-governmental cemetery in the nation.

During the Civil War, Indianapolis was a boom town, serving as a major hub for Union troop movements and Confederate prisoners of war. But the war also created a population spike for the city's main cemetery, Greenlawn. Hemmed in by factories, meat-packing plants, and railroad tracks, the cemetery had no room to expand, and the surroundings weren't exactly tranquil.

What Indianapolis needed was a cemetery like Pére Lachaise in Paris—a park-like setting outside the city that could serve as a place of rest for both the living and the dead. In 1863, a group of prominent citizens formed the Association of Crown Hill, and they hired landscape architect John Chislett. He was known for creating cemeteries in a "picturesque romantic style of an imagined English landscape, with scenic winding roads, gazing ponds, and lush glades for the contemplation of nature and eternity." Chislett soon began searching for a suitable setting. When he saw Strawberry Hill, one of the highest elevations in Marion County, he said, "That is the spot. Buy those grounds at whatever price you have to pay."

The cemetery was dedicated the following June. The *Indianapolis Sentinel* wrote, "It is surpassingly beautiful. It appeals to every noble sentiment that animates the human heart." The first person laid to rest there was Lucy Ann Seaton, a young wife who had died of tuberculosis. Since then, the cemetery has become the final resting place of President Benjamin Harrison, three vice presidents, 11 Indiana governors, Col. Eli Lilly, the poet James Whitcomb Riley, and even the notorious John Dillinger.

In Memory

Indianapolis is home to more war memorials than any other US city outside Washington, DC. The list includes the Soldiers & Sailors Monument, the Indiana War Memorial, the USS *Indianapolis* Memorial, and the Medal of Honor Memorial.

Courtesy of the Library of Congress

Courtesy of the Library of Congress

“BACKED TO WIN.”

Chapter Eight

Famous Locals

History is full of famous Hoosiers, from Johnny Appleseed and Abraham Lincoln to musician Axl Rose and actor James Dean. And many of these Hoosier celebrities hail from Indianapolis. The list includes a US president, as well as the nation's first self-made female millionaire. The "King of Cool," actor Steve McQueen, was born here, as were television personalities David Letterman and Jane Pauley. Famous athletes such as Major Taylor, Oscar Robertson, and Oscar Charleston (and many others) all called this city home, as did celebrated writer Kurt Vonnegut (and many other writers). I have omitted many other worthy candidates, and for that I apologize in advance.

President Benjamin Harrison

The Circle City's hometown president, Benjamin Harrison, was born in 1833 to a prominent political family. His great-grandfather had served as governor of Virginia, and his grandfather was President William Henry Harrison (who died of pneumonia only one month into his term). Although Harrison was born in Ohio, in his early 20s he set up a law practice in Indianapolis, where he lived for the rest of his life—with the exception of the years he spent in Washington, DC.

Early in his career, Harrison became involved in Republican politics, and he was renowned for his speeches on behalf of the party. His political life was interrupted by the Civil War, and he enlisted in the Union Army in 1862, eventually earning the rank of brigadier general. Back home after the war, he ran a losing campaign for Indiana governor, then served one term in the US Senate. Then, in 1888, he became the Republican nominee for president. He conducted a famously successful "front porch campaign," in which delegations from across the country came to Indianapolis to hear him speak. When he left the city by train for his inauguration, he said, "I love this city. It has been my own cherished home."

As president, Harrison spearheaded an ambitious legislative agenda. He signed the Sherman Anti-Trust Act of 1890, as well as a bill authorizing federal pensions for Union veterans. He also signed the Forest Reserve Act, which enabled the president to set aside public lands as national forests; he himself preserved 13 million acres. But one of his primary campaign promises, legislation to improve education and voting access for Black people in the South, never made it through Congress.

Harrison's wife, Caroline, died in 1892, just two weeks before the next election, which he lost to Grover Cleveland. Despondent, he returned to Indianapolis and rebuilt his law practice. A few years later, Harrison caused a minor scandal when he married the much younger Mary Scott Dimmick, the niece of his late wife. The marriage destroyed his relationship with his two adult children. "I freely confess that I so thoroughly despise the woman that I cannot form an unbiased opinion nor a wise one," his daughter wrote to her husband. The rift never healed. Harrison died of pneumonia in 1901, and he is buried at Crown Hill Cemetery.

Courtesy of the Library of Congress

Madam C. J. Walker

Sarah Breedlove was an unlikely millionaire. Born in 1867 on the same Louisiana plantation where her parents had been enslaved, she was orphaned at age 7, married at age 14, and widowed at age 20. The single mother worked for many years as a laundress and cook in St. Louis, where her brothers were barbers.

Courtesy of the Smithsonian National Museum of African American History and Culture

Necessity, however, is the mother of invention. When Breedlove—who had married a man named Charles Joseph Walker—developed a scalp disease in her late 30s and started to lose her hair, she developed a homemade remedy that actually worked. Word spread, and with $1.25 in capital she launched the product as Madam C. J. Walker's Wonderful Hair Grower. It was the first in a large line of beauty products for Black women, an under-served market then as now. In 1910, Walker moved her headquarters to Indianapolis to take advantage of the city's extensive shipping connections.

Walker wasn't just any millionaire; she was the first self-made female millionaire in the nation. She built a mansion in New York, where her neighbors were the Rockefeller, Vanderbilt, and Tiffany families. And she shared that prosperity by hiring women as licensed sales consultants, employing more than 40,000 people over the years. She also founded the National Negro Cosmetics Manufacturers Association.

But not even the prosperous Walker was safe from racial prejudice. One day, she visited a downtown theater and discovered that the price of admission for Black customers had increased from 15 cents to 25 cents. White customers were still charged the lower fee. An outraged Walker vowed to build her own theater instead, and she purchased a lot for that purpose on Indiana Avenue in one of the city's predominantly Black neighborhoods. The theater opened in 1927, eight years after her death, and it is now a National Historic Landmark.

A Fitting Tribute

The downtown Alexander hotel displays an unusual portrait of Walker. Created by artist Sonya Clark, the artwork is made of 3,840 black plastic hair combs.

Courtesy of the Smithsonian National Museum of African American History and Culture

Steve McQueen

On the first day of filming the TV series *Wanted: Dead or Alive*, Beech Grove native Steve McQueen fired one of his co-stars: his horse. The actor was notoriously difficult to work with, and he generally got away with it—because he was a genuine superstar. One of the highest-paid actors of the 1960s and 1970s, he made a string of blockbuster films that still stand as cultural icons. Today he is remembered as "cinema's first rock star" and the "King of Cool."

McQueen's early life was chaotic, with an absent father and alcoholic mother. As a teenager, he spent more than a year in reform school, and he once skipped town with a traveling carnival. He joined the Merchant Marine at age 16 but then defected in the Dominican Republic. Later he worked as a lumberjack and a taxi mechanic, made sandals and artificial flowers, ran errands for a bookie, and even sold encyclopedias door to door. He also spent a stint in the Marines and was court-martialed for going AWOL (although he later received an honorable discharge). But he finally found his place when he started going along with a girlfriend to her acting lessons. He was a natural.

After being accepted into the exclusive Actors Studio, McQueen picked up small roles on stage and screen. His typical character was "cool, understated, and extremely at ease with a gun in his hand or behind the wheel of a fast-moving vehicle," his biographer wrote. His first starring role was in the campy 1958 sci-fi thriller *The Blob*, and then he was cast as a Wild West bounty hunter in *Wanted: Dead or Alive*. He had a supporting role in *The Magnificent Seven*, but it was the wartime film *The Great Escape*, with its legendary motorcycle jump, that made him an international star. (He raced—and often crashed—cars and motorcycles as a hobby.)

That movie was followed by *The Cincinnati Kid*; *The Sand Pebbles*, for which he received an Oscar nod; *The Thomas Crown Affair*; and *Bullitt*,

Courtesy of the Library of Congress

known for its iconic car chase. After a few misfires, he then had a box-office smash with *The Towering Inferno*, the highest-grossing film of 1974. Then, bored of stardom and content with his success, he semi-retired from Hollywood. He died of mesothelioma in 1980, at the age of 50, and is still remembered as one of cinema's greatest stars.

Kurt Vonnegut

Indianapolis writer Kurt Vonnegut spent decades trying—and failing—to write about the defining experience of his life. Captured during the Battle of the Bulge in World War II, he was held as a prisoner of war in the German city of Dresden. In February 1945, that city was firebombed by Allied forces, resulting in more than 25,000 civilian deaths and the utter destruction of one of Europe's most beautiful cities. He and other POWs survived by sheltering in an underground meat locker. Eventually, the trauma of that experience led to Vonnegut's most successful novel, the anti-war *Slaughterhouse-Five*. He had struggled to write the novel, he said, because "there is nothing intelligent to say about a massacre."

In Indianapolis, the Vonnegut family—descended from German immigrants—was prominent long before Kurt Vonnegut made his name as a writer. His great-grandfather had founded Vonnegut Hardware, which survived for more than a century. His maternal grandfather, Albert Lieber, had been president of the Indianapolis Brewing Company. And his paternal grandfather had founded the Vonnegut and Bohn architectural firm, which designed the Athenaeum (formerly Das Deutsche Haus), the Herron School of Art, and many other prominent buildings. Kurt Vonnegut joined the family in 1922 and later attended Shortridge High School.

After the war, Vonnegut married, and he supported his growing family by working as a beat reporter in Chicago. He later took a job in the public relations department at General Electric in Schenectady, New York. And at one point he even owned a Saab dealership. In addition to raising his own three children, he and his wife, Jane, took in three of his nephews after his sister and her husband died within 36 hours of each other.

But along the way, Vonnegut was writing short stories, often using the tropes of science fiction to comment on contemporary society. He accumulated a stack of rejection letters from national magazines, but finally one of his stories—"Report on the Barnhouse Effect"—was published in the February 1950 issue of *Collier's*. It was the break he needed. His first novel, *Player Piano*, appeared two years later. The novels that followed, such as *Cat's Cradle*, *Sirens of Titan*, and eventually *Slaughterhouse-Five*, became known for their satire, dark humor, and elements of metafiction. He became a hero of the 1960s counterculture, and for the rest of his life Vonnegut was a sought-after speaker and essayist. He died in 2007.

Courtesy of Library of Congress, Prints & Photographs Division, photograph by Bernard Gotfryd

Oscar Robertson

A legendary basketball player with the nickname "The Big O," Oscar Robertson moved to Indianapolis at age 4 from rural Tennessee, where many of his ancestors had been enslaved. Living in poverty as a child, he learned to play basketball in pick-up games at Lockefield Gardens. At home on Colton Street, he practiced his shots with an imaginary hoop and a ball of rags. But "a wonderful thing about sports is that they give everyone a chance," Robertson wrote in his autobiography.

Robertson made the varsity squad at the segregated Crispus Attucks High School in his sophomore year. That year, the team lost its post-season sectional to Milan High School, whose state championship victory was immortalized in the movie *Hoosiers*. But in his junior year, Crispus Attucks easily won the state championship, the first time an Indianapolis team had claimed the title. The following season, the team was undefeated in the regular season and claimed another championship. By this

Courtesy of Wikimedia Commons

time, Robertson was regarded as one of the best high school players in the nation, and he was heavily recruited by colleges across the country.

Wanting to stay within a bus ride of home, Robertson chose the University of Cincinnati. He did not win a championship with that team, and off the court he was one of the few Black students on campus. But he was named college player of the year for three consecutive seasons, and after graduation in 1960 he made the Olympics team that won a gold medal in Rome.

Under the NBA's territorial rules at the time, Robertson was drafted by the under-performing Cincinnati Royals. He made the cover of *Time* magazine in 1961, the first basketball player to do so. And in his 1962 season he became the first player in league history to average a triple-double—double figures in points, rebounds, and assists. (The feat was not achieved again until 2016.) Roberston was later traded to the Milwaukee Bucks, where, playing alongside Kareem Abdul-Jabbar, he finally won a national championship.

Robertson made his most enduring contribution to the game, however, as president of the National Basketball Players Association. In 1970, the union filed suit to stop a proposed merger between two basketball leagues, alleging that it would create an unfair monopoly. The merger was eventually approved, but the lawsuit led to free agency, which gave players much more leverage in contract negotiations.

Major Taylor

Major Taylor, the future world champion cyclist, had an unusual childhood. He was born into poverty in Indianapolis in 1878, but at age 8 he became the companion of a wealthy boy, Dan Southard. The two boys were inseparable for five years, wearing the same clothes, attending the same lessons, and learning together to ride bicycles. Southard made sure that Taylor had a bike of his own.

Taylor's privileged life ended abruptly at age 13 when the Southards moved to Chicago . . . but he got to keep his bicycle. Soon he was working at a local bicycle shop, doing trick riding demonstrations in front of the store. One day his boss entered him into a 10-mile road race. Taylor had never even seen a bicycle race, but he won by six seconds. Soon, Taylor was winning amateur races all over the country. His opponents often called him racist names and attempted to foul him. He responded by simply getting faster; they couldn't hurt him if they couldn't catch him.

Taylor went pro in 1896, at age 18. He did well on the racing circuit in 1897, despite receiving death threats. But he was unable to finish the season because he was barred from many tracks, especially in the South.

For the 1898 season, the League of American Wheelmen—which organized the races—refused to sanction any race or track from which Taylor was barred. That season Taylor broke seven world records. And he was poised to win the league championship when many of the cyclists suddenly revolted and refused to compete.

Taylor continued to break records the following season, and he quickly became a fan favorite. He won the one-mile world championship in Montreal that August—making him only the second Black person to hold a world championship in any sport. He easily won back-to-back league championships in 1899 and 1900. And in 1901 he toured Europe, placing first in 18 of the 24 races in which he competed.

Taylor continued touring until his retirement in 1910. The cycling craze was over by then, and bicycle races were no longer drawing big crowds. Taylor was largely forgotten, and he died penniless in 1932. Recently, however, Taylor has received increasing attention. The velodrome at Marian University is named in his honor, and a five-story mural on Washington Street now celebrates his legacy as one of the city's most successful athletes.

Courtesy of Wikimedia Commons

Oscar Charleston

The *Chicago Defender* once referred to a certain baseball player as "the greatest player in the world," but the newspaper wasn't talking about Babe Ruth, Hank Aaron, or Willie Mays. The focus of the article was Oscar Charleston. Because he was Black, Charleston was barred from playing in the major leagues at the time. But in the Negro Leagues, the Hoosier nevertheless carved out a legendary career.

Born in Indianapolis in 1896, Charleston grew up in the predominantly Black neighborhoods of Martindale and Indiana Avenue. He played sandlot games and worked as a batboy, but his real introduction to baseball came at age 15, when he lied about his age to join the army. Stationed in the Philippines, Charleston played for his regiment's team in the local league, and he quickly set himself apart.

Three years later, Charleston received an honorable discharge and joined the Indianapolis ABCs, one of the strongest teams in the Negro Leagues. It was an on-again-off-again relationship. In the early years of his career, Charleston also played for the Harlem-based Lincoln Stars, the Chicago American Giants, and the St. Louis Giants. Although he developed a reputation for fighting on the field, he also became known for his "miraculous" catches in center field and for all-around excellent play. Statistics for the Negro Leagues are incomplete, but Charleston appears to have posted the best numbers in league history.

In 1924, Charleston joined the Harrisburg Giants as both player and manager. By then he was one of the best-paid athletes in the league. Still, a reporter once found him taking correspondence courses in fingerprinting to prepare for the future. Having grown up in poverty, he never took the money for granted.

In 1932, Charleston was named manager of the Pittsburgh Crawfords. He stayed with the team for seven years and there won his first managerial championship. He later managed the Philadelphia Stars. And in 1954 he came home, becoming the manager of the Indianapolis Clowns. The team traveled with actual clowns and pulled stunts to wow the crowds, but they also played excellent baseball. Charleston led the team to a league championship.

Charleston died of cancer later that year, and for decades he was largely forgotten. In 1976, however, he was finally inducted into the Baseball Hall of Fame. He may well have been the greatest baseball player of all time.

Courtesy of the National Baseball Hall of Fame and Museum, Cooperstown, NY

David Letterman

Born in Indianapolis in 1947, David Letterman—the future king of late-night television—was destined for an offbeat broadcasting career. As a child he hosted a fake talk show in his basement. As a telecommunications student at Ball State University, he worked at the campus radio station, sneaking on the air after midnight to play rock and roll on the classical station. Moved to the station's news department, he made up fake reports about, for example, the International Fungo Ball League. "Letterman's quintessential joke was the benign lie," wrote a biographer. Eventually Letterman was fired.

After graduation, Letterman returned to Indianapolis, where he worked as a weekend weatherman and hosted a children's television show. But his father had died young, and Letterman didn't want to waste any time. In 1975 he moved to Los Angeles to become a television writer and stand-up comedian.

Letterman had a few early failures in Hollywood, but in 1978 he did a well-received stand-up comedy routine on the *Tonight Show with Johnny Carson*. He later made regular appearances on the show, serving several times as a guest host. The following year, the network offered him his own daytime talk show, the *David Letterman Show*. It was "a chaotic and cluttered mess," wrote one biographer, and it was canceled after only four months. But the show debuted segments such as "Stupid Pet Tricks" that later became favorites on his late-night programs.

Late Night with David Letterman—which aired immediately after the *Tonight Show*—debuted in 1982. Known for its "ironic and offbeat humor," it received five Emmy Awards and 35 nominations. When Carson announced his retirement from the *Tonight Show* 10 years later, everyone—including Carson—assumed that Letterman would replace him. Instead, NBC gave the job to Jay Leno.

Courtesy of the Library of Congress, Prints & Photographs Division, photograph by Bernard Gotfryd

In 1993, CBS capitalized on the drama by creating the *Late Show with David Letterman*, which aired in the same timeslot as the *Tonight Show*. The two shows had an intense ratings rivalry for more than two decades. In 2012, Letterman celebrated 30 years as a late-night talk-show host, the longest tenure in American television history. He announced his retirement from the show three years later, but his work continued with projects such as Netflix's *My Next Guest Needs No Introduction*.

Jane Pauley

Jane Pauley and Tom Brokaw on the set of *Today* in 1977
Courtesy of Wikimedia Commons

Jane Pauley was a student at Warren Central High School when she experienced what was, to her, a devastating blow—she failed to make the cheerleading squad. Instead, the disappointed teenager turned her attention to speech and debate competitions, which set her on the path to her future career as one of the nation's most prominent television journalists.

After graduating from Indiana University in 1972, Pauley got a tryout for WISH-TV in Indianapolis. Hired as a reporter, she quickly earned a promotion to news anchor. It was the beginning of a meteoric rise. In 1975, Pauley was recruited to Chicago's NBC affiliate and became the first woman in the city to anchor a weekday evening newscast. She was unprepared for the public expectations of the role. Once, when asked whose dress she was wearing, she naively responded, "Mine."

At the same time, the legendary Barbara Walters announced that she was leaving *Today*, and the search for her replacement became a media event of its own. Pauley was only 25, with only a few years of experience, so she was as surprised as anyone when *Today* offered her the role. But she had "the talent to come across as warm and sincere and wholesome on television," she wrote in her memoir, and she co-anchored the popular morning news show from 1976 to 1989. Her departure caused a media frenzy: Was she being fired to make way for a younger woman? Pauley, however, maintains that leaving the show was her decision.

Later in her career, Pauley had a couple of flops—*Real Life with Jane Pauley* and a daytime talk show, both of which were canceled after one season. But she also served as founding co-anchor of the successful and influential *Dateline*, a role she held from 1992 to 2003. She later returned to *Today* for weekly guest segments.

In 2014, Pauley appeared in a "where are they now" segment on *CBS News Sunday Morning*. Audience response to the episode was so positive that Pauley was asked to join the team, and two years later she became the show's host. She has now spent more than half a century in the spotlight, yet she is still perceived by viewers as a regular girl next door.

Endnotes

Invented Here

Barbasol Shaving Cream

"Frank B. Shields, 62, Headed Barbasol Co." *New York Times*, 17 October 1946, p. 22.

Markisohn, Deborah B. and Elizabeth J. Van Allen. "Barbasol." *Encyclopedia of Indianapolis.* indyencyclopedia.org/barbasol.

Mitchell, Dawn. "RetroIndy: A Close Shave with Barbasol." *Indianapolis Star*, 15 September 2017. indystar.com/story/news/history/retroindy/2017/09/15/retroindy-close-shave-barbasol/662662001.

"Our History." Barbasol. barbasol.com/pages/our-history.

Wonder Bread

Advertisements. *Indianapolis Star*, 23 May 1921, 1 June 1921, 3 September 1921, and 26 October 1921.

Hyman, Max R., Ed. *Hyman's Hand Book of Indianapolis.* Indianapolis: M. R. Hyman Company, 1907.

Sulgrove, B. R. *History of Indianapolis and Marion County, Indiana.* Philadelphia: L. H. Everts & Co., 1884.

The Wonder Bread Cookbook. Berkeley: Ten Speed Press, 2007.

Sliced Bacon

Donnelly, Cathleen F. "Kingan & Co." The *Encyclopedia of Indianapolis.* indyencyclopedia.org/kingan-and-company.

Dunn, Jacob Piatt. *Greater Indianapolis: The History, the Industries, the Institutions, and the People of a City of Homes.* Vol. I. Chicago: The Lewis Publishing Company, 1910, p. 349.

Holloway, W. R. *Indianapolis: A Historical and Statistical Sketch of the Railroad City.* Indianapolis: *Indianapolis Journal* Printers, 1870, p. 129.

Hyman, Max R., Ed. *Hyman's Hand Book of Indianapolis.* Indianapolis: M. R. Hyman Company, 1897, pp. 119, 272.

Sulgrove, B. R. *History of Indianapolis and Marion County, Indiana.* Philadelphia: L. H. Everts & Co., 1884, pp. 444-446.

Tenuth, Jeffrey. *Indianapolis: A Circle City History.* Charleston, SC: Arcadia Publishing, 2004, pp. 58-59.

Raggedy Ann and Raggedy Andy

Hall, Patricia. "Raggedy Ann and Andy: History and Legend." Raggedy Land, 1999. raggedy-ann.com/patty.html.

Johnson, Leigh Anne. "Johnny Gruelle and Raggedy Ann." Indiana State Library, 5 October 2016, blog.library.in.gov/johnny-gruelle-and-raggedy-ann.

Lodge, Sally. "Raggedy Ann Turns 100." *Publishers Weekly*, 22 September 2015, publishersweekly.com/pw/by-topic/childrens/childrens-book-news/article/68132-at-100-raggedy-ann-embodies-a-creative-family-legacy.html.

The Vajen-Bader Smoke Protector

Hyman, Max R., Ed. *Hyman's Hand Book of Indianapolis.* Indianapolis: M. R. Hyman Company, 1897, p. 343.

"Protection for Firemen: A Fireproof Helmet with an Air Reservoir." *Los Angeles Herald*, 31 March 1895, p. 11.

"Secure Against Smoke." *Salt Lake Herald*, 10 August 1896, p. 8.

Taylor, Stephen J. "That Foulsome Air May Do No Harm." *Hoosier State Chronicles*, 23 April 2015. blog.newspapers.library.in.gov/that-foulsome-air-may-do-no-harm.

The First Machine Gun

"About People and Things." *Indianapolis Journal*, 24 March 1884, p. 4.

Sanford, Wayne L. and Elizabeth J. Van Allen. "Gatling Gun." *Encyclopedia of Indianapolis*, indyencyclopedia.org/gatling-gun.

"The Gatling Gun." *Indianapolis Journal*, 2 April 1884, p. 2.

Towne, Stephen E. "Richard J. Gatling." *Encyclopedia of Indianapolis*, indyencyclopedia.org/richard-j-gatling.

The Rearview Mirror

Davidson, Donald, and Rick Shaffer. *Official History of the Indianapolis 500.* Hong Kong: Icon Publishing Ltd., 2013.

Williams, Casey. "A Century of Indy 500 Innovations: From Track to Street." WFYI, 4 May 2016, wfyi.org/news/articles/a-century-of-indy-500-innovations--from-track-to-street.

The Transistor Radio

Schiffer, Michael Brian. *The Portable Radio in American Life.* Tucson and London: University of Arizona Press, 1991.

Simcoe, Robert J. "The Revolution in Your Pocket." *American Heritage of Invention & Technology*, fall 2004, pp. 12-18.

Eli Lilly's Insulin Breakthrough

"Celebrating the First Century of the World's First Life-Saving Drug." Eli Lilly & Co. lilly.com/discovery/100-years-of-insulin/timeline.

Hyman, Max R., Ed. *Hyman's Hand Book of Indianapolis.* Indianapolis: M. R. Hyman Company, 1897.

Madison, James H. *Eli Lilly: A Life*, 1885-1977. Indianapolis: Indiana Historical Society, 1989.

Sidebar: Kobrowski, Nicole R. *Fractured Intentions: A History of Central State Hospital for the Insane.* Westfield, Indiana: Unseen Press, 2014.

Overlooked Locals

The Ragtime Composer: May Frances Aufderheide

Morath, Max. "May Aufderheide and the Ragtime Women." *Ragtime: Its History, Composers, and Music.* Ed. John Edward Hasse. New York: Schirmer Books, 1985, pp. 154-165.

Vanderstel, Sheryl D. "May Frances Aufderheide." *Encyclopedia of Indianapolis.* Ed. David J. Bodenhamer and Robert G. Barrows. Bloomington and Indianapolis: Indiana University Press, 1994, p. 272.

Sidebar: "Take Me Out to the Ball Game." Songwriters Hall of Fame, 2008. songhall.org/awards/winner/take_me_out_to_the_ball_game.

The Writer: Meredith Nicholson

Gray, Ralph D. *Meredith Nicholson: A Writing Life.* Indianapolis: Indiana Historical Society Press, 2007.

Gray, Ralph D. "Meredith Nicholson." *Encyclopedia of Indianapolis*, indyencyclopedia.org/meredith-nicholson.

"Meredith Nicholson 1866-1947." Indiana Historical Bureau. in.gov/history/state-historical-markers/find-a-marker/find-historical-markers-by-county/indiana-historical-markers-by-county/meredith-nicholson-1866-1947.

The Humorist: Kin Hubbard

Boomhower, Ray. "Frank McKinney (Kin) Hubbard." *Encyclopedia of Indianapolis*, indyencyclopedia.org/frank-mckinney-kin-hubbard.

Boomhower, Ray. *Indiana Originals: Hoosier Heroes & Heroines.* Charleston, SC: The History Press, 2018.

"Kin Hubbard, Abe Martin Creator, Dies at His Home." *Indianapolis Star*, 27 December 1930, pp. 1-2.

The Fighter: Madge Oberholtzer

Moore, Leonard J., and James H. Madison. "Ku Klux Klan." *Encyclopedia of Indianapolis*, indyencyclopedia.org/ku-klux-klan.

Ottinger, Charlotte Halsema. *Madge.* Indianapolis: Irvington Historical Society Press, 2021.

The Police Officer: William Whitfield

"Believe Woman Saw Cop Shot." *Indianapolis Star*, 20 June 1922, p. 1.

"Negro Cop Shot by White Man." *Indianapolis Star*, 19 June 1922, p. 1.

Sharp, Wayne. *Legends in Blue.* USA: Hawthorne Publishing, 2002.

The Police Officer: Emma Christy Baker

"Emma Christy Baker." Indiana Commission for Women. in.gov/icw/files/20170316-Baker,-Emma-Christy.pdf and in.gov/icw/files/2015-03-22_Emma_Christy_Baker.pdf.

Pearsey, Patrick. "Emma Christy Baker." *Encyclopedia of Indianapolis.* indyencyclopedia.org/emma-christy-baker.

Spalding, Tom. "Police Legend Revered at Last." *Indianapolis Star*, 20 June 2003, pp. B1, B7.

Sidebar: "City's First Woman Firefighter Resigns." *Indianapolis Star*, 22 August 1979, p. 33.

Rubinton, Noel. "City on Verge of Having Its First Female Firefighter." *Indianapolis Star*, 13 February 1978, pp. 1, 4.

Rubinton, Noel. "Fire Department Swears in First Woman." *Indianapolis Star*, 4 March 1978, pp. 1, 5.

Witkin, Gordon. "City Fires Its Female Firefighter for Tardiness, 'Lack of Interest.'" *Indianapolis Star*, 14 October 1978, pp. 1, 15.

"Woman Fire Fighter Reinstated by Board." *Indianapolis Star*, 25 May 1979, p. 26.

The Soldier: Walter Bedell Smith

Bakken, Dawn E. *On This Day in Indianapolis History.* Charleston, SC: The History Press, 2016, p. 169.

Bishop, James R. "Walter Bedell (Beetle) Smith." *Encyclopedia of Indianapolis*, indyencyclopedia.org/walter-bedell-beetle-smith.

Dujmovic, Nicholas. "The Significance of Walter Bedell Smith as Director of Central Intelligence, 1950-53." Central Intelligence Agency, cia.gov/readingroom/docs/misc-009.pdf.

Hymel, Kevin M. "'Beetle' Smith and the Surrender of Nazi Germany." Arlington National Cemetery, 8 May 2020, arlingtoncemetery.mil/blog/post/10742/beetle-smith-and-the-surrender-of- nazi-germany.

"Walter Bedell Smith." *Britannica*, britannica.com/biography/walter-bedell-smith.

The Artist: Felrath Hines

Perry, Rachel Berenson. "Felrath Hines." *Encyclopedia of Indianapolis*, indyencyclopedia.org/felrath-hines.

Perry, Rachel Berenson. "Felrath Hines—Bio." felrathhines.com/bio.

Perry, Rachel Berenson. *The Life and Art of Felrath Hines.* Bloomington, Indiana: Indiana University Press, 2018.

The Crooners: The Ink Spots

Nooger, Dan. "The Ink Spots." Rock and Roll Hall of Fame. rockhall.com/wp-content/uploads/2024/03/The_Ink_Spots_1989.pdf

Verderame, Jyoti A. "The Ink Spots." *Encyclopedia of Indianapolis.* indyencyclopedia.org/the-ink-spots.

The Criminal Element

The Christmas Jailbreak

Dunn, Jacob Piatt. *Greater Indianapolis: The History, the Industries, the Institutions, and the People of a City of Homes.* Chicago: Lewis Publishing Company, 1910, pp. 47-48.

Holloway, W. R. *Indianapolis: A Historical and Statistical Sketch of the Railroad City.* Indianapolis: *Indianapolis Journal* Printers, 1870, p. 12.

Sulgrove, B. R. *History of Indianapolis and Marion County, Indiana.* Philadelphia: L. H. Everts & Co., 1884, p. 34.

Sidebar: Stoner, Andrew E. *Wanted in Indiana: Infamous Hoosier Fugitives.* Charleston, SC: The History Press, 2021, pp. 11-14.

Burkhart and the Chain Gang

Dunn, Jacob Piatt. *Greater Indianapolis: The History, the Industries, the Institutions, and the People of a City of Homes.* Vol. I. Chicago: The Lewis Publishing Company, 1910, pp. 114-116.

Holloway, W. R. *Indianapolis: A Historical and Statistical Sketch of the Railroad City.* Indianapolis: *Indianapolis Journal* Printers, 1870, p. 53.

Sulgrove, B. R. *History of Indianapolis and Marion County, Indiana.* Philadelphia: L. H. Everts & Co., 1884, pp. 48-49.

Thornbrough, Gayle, ed. *The Diary of Calvin Fletcher: Vol. 1, 1817-1838.* Indianapolis: Indiana Historical Society, 1972, pp. 322-339.

The Antics of the Volunteer Firefighters

Indianapolis Fire Department: 1859-2009. Evansville, IN: M. T. Publishing Company, Inc., 2011.

Double Murder Leads to Media Frenzy

Cavinder, Fred D. *Historic Indianapolis Crimes.* Charleston, SC: The History Press, 2010, pp. 46-51.

Gamber, Wendy. *The Notorious Mrs. Clem: Murder and Money in the Gilded Age.* Baltimore: Johns Hopkins University Press, 2016.

Hyman, Max R., Ed. *Hyman's Hand Book of Indianapolis.* Indianapolis: M. R. Hyman Company, 1897, p. 50.

Sulgrove, B. R. *History of Indianapolis and Marion County, Indiana.* Philadelphia: L. H. Everts & Co., 1884, pp. 42-43.

The Grave-Robbing Conspiracy

Beckley, Lindsey. "'King of Ghouls' Rufus Cantrell & Grave-Robbing in Indianapolis." Untold Indiana. Indiana Historical Bureau, 31 October 2020, blog.history.in.gov/king-of-ghouls-rufus-cantrell-grave-robbing-in-indianapolis.

Flook, Chris. *Indianapolis Graverobbing: A Syndicate of Death.* Charleston, SC: The History Press, 2023.

"Grave Robbing Scandal." Indiana Historical Bureau. in.gov/history/state-historical-markers/find-a-marker/find-historical-markers-by-county/indiana-historical-markers-by-county/grave-robbing-scandal.

The Murder of Dr. Knabe

Cavinder, Fred D. *Historic Indianapolis Crimes.* Charleston, SC: The History Press, 2010.

Kobrowski, Nicole R. *She Sleeps Well: The Extraordinary Life and Murder of Dr. Helene Elise Hermine Knabe.* Westfield, Indiana: Unseen Press, 2016.

The 1913 Police Mutiny

"33 Patrolmen Are Suspended." *Indianapolis Star*, 14 November 1913, p. 1.

"Car Men Fail to Win Recognition and Call Strike." *Indianapolis Star*, 1 November 1913, p. 1.

"Car Service Is at Standstill; No Steps Taken." *Indianapolis Star*, 2 November 1913, p. 1.

"Charges Faced by 33 Officers." *Indianapolis Star*, 13 November 1913, p. 16.

"Deputy Sheriffs Will Aid Police in Strike Duty." *Indianapolis Star*, 3 November 1913, p. 1.

"Shank Defends Patrolmen Who Ignored Orders." *Indianapolis Star*, 22 November 1913, p. 1.

Stoner, Andrew E. *Wicked Indianapolis.* Charleston, SC: The History Press, 2011.

Zeigler, Connie J. "Street Railway Strikes." *Encyclopedia of Indianapolis*, indyencyclopedia.org/street-railway-strikes.

Pharmacists or Bootleggers?

"Charges Haags Operated 'Most Vicious Tiger.'" *Indiana Daily Times*, 21 June 1920, pp. 1-2.

"Federal Court Indicts Haags." *Indianapolis Star*, 5 May 1920, p. 3.

"Haag Brothers Begin Sentence at Penal Farm." *Indianapolis Star*, 9 February 1921, p. 1.

"Haag Brothers Out on Parole, Arrive in City." *Indianapolis Star*, 4 February 1921, p. 1.

"Haags Sentenced." *Indiana Daily Times*, 23 June 1920, pp. 1-2.

Markisohn, Deborah B. "Haag Drug Company." *Encyclopedia of Indianapolis*, indyencyclopedia.org/haag-drug-company-1876-1979.

Mitchell, Dawn. "Cut Price Drugs: Remembering Haag Drug, Your Neighborhood Pharmacy." *Indianapolis Star*, 22 November 2019, indystar.com/story/news/history/retroindy/2019/11/22/haag-drug-indianapolis-drugstore/4193407002.

Our Homegrown Gangster

"City Bank Robbed; Hunt Gang in Muncie." *Indianapolis Star*, 7 September 1933, p. 1.

"Four Name Man as City Bank Robber." *Indianapolis Star*, 23 September 1933, p. 1.

"John Dillinger." Federal Bureau of Investigation. fbi.gov/history/famous-cases/john-dillinger.

Rex, Aimee L. "John Herbert Dillinger." *Encyclopedia of Indianapolis*, indyencyclopedia.org/john-herbert-dillinger.

Stoner, Andrew E. "John Dillinger on His Home Turf." *Wicked Indianapolis.* Charleston, SC: The History Press, 2007, pp. 35-37.

The Marjorie Jackson Murder

"Biggest Robbery in US History Ends in Murder." *Indianapolis Star*, 15 May 1977, p. 53, 66.

Cunningham. Joan. "Marjorie Jackson Murder Case." *Encyclopedia of Indianapolis*, indyencyclopedia.org/marjorie-jackson-murder-case.

"Fast Detective Work." *Indianapolis Star*, 12 May 1977, p. 43.

LaMarche, Robert J. "Grocery Heiress Found Slain." *Indianapolis Star*, 8 May 1977, p. 1, 17.

LaMarche, Robert J. "Pair Nabbed in Jackson Slaying." *Indianapolis Star*, 21 May 1977, p. 1.

Pickering, Carolyn. "A Recluse Heiress Who Mistrusted Banks." *Indianapolis Star*, 15 May 1977, p. 53, 66.

Pickering, Carolyn. "Robinson Innocent of Jackson Slaying; Guilty on Other Counts." *Indianapolis Star*, 25 April 1978, p. 1.

The Burger Chef Murders

Cavinder, Fred D. *Historic Indianapolis Crimes: Murder and Mystery in the Circle City*. Charleston, SC: The History Press, 2010.

Young, Julie. *The Burger Chef Murders in Indiana*. Charleston, SC: The History Press, 2019.

Sidebar: Stoner, Andrew E. *Wicked Indianapolis*. Charleston, SC: The History Press, 2011.

The Kiritsis Hostage Crisis

Hall, Dick, and Lisa Hendrickson. *Kiritsis and Me: Enduring 63 Hours at Gunpoint*. Evansville, Indiana: M. T. Publishing Company, 2017.

Stoner, Andrew E. *Wicked Indianapolis*. Charleston, SC: The History Press, 2011, pp. 39-42.

Our Homegrown Serial Killer

Allen, Jake. "Victims of Fox Hollow Farm to Be Remembered." *Indianapolis Star*, 24 August 2024, p. 1.

Estep, Richard, and Robert Graves. *The Horrors of Fox Hollow Farm*. Woodbury, MN: Llewellyn Publications, 2019.

LaBalme, Jenny. "Suicide Note Mentions Marriage, Business but Not Bones." *Indianapolis Star*, 6 July 1996, p. 1.

Sidebar: Cierzniak, Libby. "The Devil in the Circle City." Historic Indianapolis, 18 August 2012, historicindianapolis.com/indianapolis-collected-the-devil-in-the-circle-city.

The Kmart Toothpaste Bomb

Caleca, Vic. "Blast Leaves Girl's Family Reeling." *Indianapolis Star*, 19 April 1989, pp. 1, 10.

Patterson, James L. "Dead Teen Linked to K Mart Bomb." *Indianapolis Star*, 25 April, 1990, pp. 1, 8.

Patterson, James L. "IU Medical Student Reacted Instinctively." *Indianapolis Star*, 18 April 1989, pp. 1, 5.

Patterson, James L. and Vic Caleca. "Bomb Injures 5-Year-Old in K Mart." *Indianapolis Star*, 18 April 1989, pp. 1, 5.

Sikich, Chris. "Firefighter Gives Long-Awaited Hug." *Indianapolis Star*, 16 January 2018, p. 1.

Stoner, Andrew E. *Wicked Indianapolis*. Charleston, SC: The History Press, 2011.

Lost Industries

The Coney Island of the Midwest

Zeigler, Connie J. "Indianapolis Amusement Parks, 1903-1911: Landscapes on the Edge." MA diss., Indiana University, 2007.

The Hoosier House

Holloway, W. R. *Indianapolis: A Historical and Statistical Sketch of the Railroad City*. Indianapolis: Indianapolis Journal Printers, 1870, pp. 368-369.

Hyman, Max R., Ed. *Hyman's Hand Book of Indianapolis*. Indianapolis: M. R. Hyman Company, 1897, p. 310.

Hyman, Max R., Ed. *Hyman's Hand Book of Indianapolis*. Indianapolis: M. R. Hyman Company, 1907, pp. 198-200.

Schrader, Richard J., ed. *The Hoosier House: Bobbs-Merrill and Its Predecessors, 1850-1985: A Documentary Volume*. Detroit: Thomson Gale, 2004.

Wagons and Wheels

Darbee, Leigh. "Woodburn Sarven Wheel Company." *Encyclopedia of Indianapolis*. Ed. David J. Bodenhamer and Robert G. Barrows. Bloomington and Indianapolis: Indiana University Press, 1994, pp. 1451-1452.

Holloway, W. R. *Indianapolis: A Historical and Statistical Sketch of the Railroad City*. Indianapolis: Indianapolis Journal Printers, 1870.

Hyman, Max R., Ed. *Hyman's Hand Book of Indianapolis*. Indianapolis: M. R. Hyman Company, 1897.

Sulgrove, B. R. *History of Indianapolis and Marion County, Indiana*. Philadelphia: L. H. Everts & Co., 1884.

Sidebar: Zeigler, Connie J. "Daniel Glazier." The *Encyclopedia of Indianapolis*. indyencyclopedia.org/daniel-glazier.

Bicycle Manufacturing

Hale, Hester Anne. *Indianapolis: The First Century*. Indianapolis: Marion County/Indianapolis Historical Society, 1987.

Hyman, Max R., Ed. *Hyman's Hand Book of Indianapolis*. Indianapolis: M. R. Hyman Company, 1897.

Ritchie, Andrew. *Mayor Taylor: "The Fastest Bicycle Rider in the World."* San Francisco: Cycle Publishing/Van Der Plas Publications, 2010.

Early Auto Manufacturing

Conant, Alan and Elizabeth J. Van Allen. "Stutz." *Encyclopedia of Indianapolis*, indyencyclopedia.org/stutz.

Guide, William F. "Marmon Automobile." *Encyclopedia of Indianapolis*, indyencyclopedia.org/marmon-automobile-1902-1933.

Hale, Hester Anne. *Indianapolis: The First Century*. Indianapolis: Marion County/Indianapolis Historical Society, 1987.

McDonald, John P. *Lost Indianapolis*. Charleston, SC: Arcadia Publishing, 2002.

Owings, Frank N., Jr., and Elizabeth J. Van Allen. "Cole Motor Car Company." *Encyclopedia of Indianapolis*, indyencyclopedia.org/cole-motor-car-company-1909-1925.

Tenuth, Jeffrey. *Indianapolis: A Circle City History*. Charleston, SC: Arcadia Publishing, 2004.

Vanderstel, Sheryl D. and Gregg Buttermore. "Fred S. Duesenberg and August S. Duesenberg." *Encyclopedia of Indianapolis*, indyencyclopedia.org/fred-s-duesenberg-and-august-s-augie-duesenberg.

Indianapolis Brewing Company

Bilger, Nathan. "Indianapolis Brewing Company." Historic Indianapolis, 1 March 2011, historicindianapolis.com/indianapolis-brewing-company.

Hedeen, Jane. "The Road to Prohibition in Indiana." Indiana Historical Society, 2011.

Hyman, Max R., Ed. *Hyman's Hand Book of Indianapolis*. Indianapolis: M. R. Hyman Company, 1907, pp. 290-292.

Peterson, Whitney. "Indianapolis Brewing Company." *Encyclopedia of Indianapolis*, indyencyclopedia.org/indianapolis-brewing-company.

Talley, James C. and Rita Kohn. "Brewing Industry." *Encyclopedia of Indianapolis*, indyencyclopedia.org/brewing-industry.

An Experiment in Democracy

Colburn Jr., Kenneth. "Columbia Conserve Company." *Encyclopedia of Indianapolis*, indyencyclopedia.org/columbia-conserve-company-1903-1953.

Hapgood, William P. *The Columbia Conserve Company: An Experiment in Workers' Management and Ownership*. Philadelphia: Porcupine Press, 1975.

The World Makers

Adams, Joe. "Changing the Face of the Globe." *Indianapolis Star* Magazine, 16 October 1955, p. 28.

"George F. Cram Company, Inc." Harvard University Collection of Historical Scientific Instruments. waywiser.fas.harvard.edu/people/4001/george-f-cram-company-inc.

Markisohn, Deborah B. "George F. Cram Company." *Encyclopedia of Indianapolis*. Ed. David J. Bodenhamer and Robert G. Barrows. Bloomington and Indianapolis: Indiana University Press, 1994, pp. 614-615.

Roberts, Richard. "Map-Making Business Soars with War Crises." *Indianapolis Star*, 4 February 1951, p. 14.

Drumroll, Please

"Band Instrument Companies Merge." *Indianapolis Star*, 4 August 1929, p. 28.

Cangany, Dan. *Mr. Leedy and the House of Wonder*. Anaheim Hills, CA: CenterStream Publishing, 2008.

Carr Childs-Helton, Sally. "Leedy Manufacturing Company." *Encyclopedia of Indianapolis*, indyencyclopedia.org/leedy-manufacturing-company.

Early, Robert. "Leedy Company Boasts World's Largest Drum Factory; Manufactures Nine Hundred Articles." *Indianapolis Star*, 19 May 1929, p. 74.

Mushlitz, Earl. "Leedy Company Business Gains." *Indianapolis Star*, 16 April 1928, pp. 1-2.

"U. G. Leedy, Nationally Known as Drum Manufacturer, Dies." *Indianapolis Star*, 8 January 1931, p. 9.

Sidebar: "Vibraphone." Britannica. britannica.com/art/vibraphone.

L. S. Ayres

McDonald, John P. *Lost Indianapolis*. Chicago: Arcadia Publishing, 2002.

Turchi, Kenneth L. *L. S. Ayres and Company: The Store at the Crossroads of America*. Indianapolis: Indiana Historical Society Press, 2012.

The Downfall of Roselyn Bakeries

Albert, Barb. "Health Fears Close Down Roselyn Plant." *Indianapolis Star*, 2 July 1999, pp. 1-2.

Clark, Jeffrey A. "A Letter from Roselyn Bakeries." *Indianapolis Star*, 8 July 1999, p. 17.

Fahy, Joe. "Roselyn Bakeries Will Cease Operations." *Indianapolis Star*, 7 August 1999, p. 1.

Roselyn Cookbook. Indianapolis: Litho Press, Inc., n.d.

Verderame, Jyoti A. "Roselyn Bakery." *Encyclopedia of Indianapolis*, indyencyclopedia.org/roselyn-bakery.

Pure Weirdness

The Great Squirrel Invasion of 1822

Johnson, Howard. *A Home in the Woods: Pioneer Life in Indiana*. Bloomington, IN: Indiana University Press, 1951, pp. 79-80.

Leary, Edward A. *Indianapolis: The Story of a City*. Indianapolis: The Bobbs-Merrill Company, 1971, p. 24.

Nolan, Jeannette Covert. *Hoosier City: The Story of Indianapolis*. New York: Julian Messner, Inc., 1943, pp. 62-63.x

Thornbrough, Gayle, ed. *The Diary of Calvin Fletcher: Vol. 1, 1817-1838.* Indianapolis: Indiana Historical Society, 1972, p. 88.

The Smiths' Theatrical Disaster

Bolton, Nathaniel. *Early History of Indianapolis and Central Indiana.* Indianapolis: The Bowen-Merrill Company, 1897, pp. 167-168.

Holloway, W. R. *Indianapolis: A Historical and Statistical Sketch of the Railroad City.* Indianapolis: Indianapolis Journal Printers, 1870, pp. 23, 146.

Leary, Edward A. *Indianapolis: The Story of a City.* Indianapolis: The Bobbs-Merrill Company, 1971, p. 26.

Sulgrove, B. R. *History of Indianapolis and Marion County, Indiana.* Philadelphia: L. H. Everts & Co., 1884, pp. 53-54.

Thornbrough, Gayle, ed. *The Diary of Calvin Fletcher: Vol. 1, 1817-1838.* Indianapolis: Indiana Historical Society, 1972, pp. 101-102.

Indy's First "Exorcism"

Sulgrove, B. R. *History of Indianapolis and Marion County, Indiana.* Philadelphia: L. H. Everts & Co., 1884, pp. 88-89.

The "Indian Doctor"

"Doctor Fryer: The Indian Doctor." *New Orleans Crescent*, 1 May 1851, p. 4.

"Dr. Fryer." *Indiana State Sentinel*, 13 November 1851, p. 2

Dunn, Jacob Piatt. *Greater Indianapolis: The History, the Industries, the Institutions, and the People of a City of Homes.* Vol. I. Chicago: The Lewis Publishing Company, 1910, p. 546.

"Sanative House." Monroe Democrat, 30 June 1852, p. 3.

Taylor, Stephen J. "The Notorious and Diamond-Bedecked Dr. Lighthall." *Hoosier State Chronicles*, 2 February 2016, blog.newspapers.library.in.gov/the-notorious-and-diamond-bedecked-dr-lighthall.

"W. F. K. Fryer, Indian Doctor." *New Orleans Crescent*, 16 February 1854, p. 4.

The Farce of the *Robert Hanna*

Dunn, Jacob Piatt. *Greater Indianapolis: The History, the Industries, the Institutions, and the People of a City of Homes.* Vol. I. Chicago: The Lewis Publishing Company, 1910, pp. 18-19.

Holloway, W. R. *Indianapolis: A Historical and Statistical Sketch of the Railroad City.* Indianapolis: *Indianapolis Journal* Printers, 1870, pp. 39-40.

Nolan, Jeannette Covert. *Hoosier City: The Story of Indianapolis.* New York: Julian Messner, Inc., 1943, pp. 88-92.

Sulgrove, B. R. *History of Indianapolis and Marion County, Indiana.* Philadelphia: L. H. Everts & Co., 1884, p. 106.

The Curse of the Governor's Mansion

Dunn, Jacob Piatt. *Greater Indianapolis: The History, the Industries, the Institutions, and the People of a City of Homes.* Vol. I. Chicago: The Lewis Publishing Company, 1910, p. 109.

Holloway, W. R. *Indianapolis: A Historical and Statistical Sketch of the Railroad City.* Indianapolis: Indianapolis Journal Printers, 1870, p. 64.

Hyman, Max R., Ed. *Hyman's Hand Book of Indianapolis.* Indianapolis: M. R. Hyman Company, 1897, p. 38.

Sulgrove, B. R. *History of Indianapolis and Marion County, Indiana.* Philadelphia: L. H. Everts & Co., 1884, p. 122.

The Irvington School War

Clarke, Grace Julian. "Irvington School War Recalled by Former Pupil." *Indianapolis Star*, 22 November 1925, p. 13.

Dunn, Jacob Piatt. *Greater Indianapolis: The History, the Industries, the Institutions, and the People of a City of Homes.* Vol. I. Chicago: The Lewis Publishing Company, 1910, pp. 435-436.

Nolan, Jeannette Covert. *Hoosier City: The Story of Indianapolis.* New York: Julian Messner, Inc., 1943, pp. 197-198.

"School Battle Livened Suburb." *Indianapolis Star*, 7 November 1971, p. 14.

The Poster Family for Eugenics

Deutsch, Nathaniel. *Inventing America's "Worst" Family.* Berkeley: University of California Press, 2009.

Forbes, J. Thomas, and Katherine Badertscher. "Oscar Carleton McCulloch." *Encyclopedia of Indianapolis*, indyencyclopedia.org/oscar-carleton-mcculloch.

Horton, Robert, and Katherine Badertscher. "Tribe of Ishmael." *Encyclopedia of Indianapolis*, indyencyclopedia.org/tribe-of-ishmael.

McCulloch, Oscar C. "The Tribe of Ishmael: A Study in Social Degradation." Internet Archive, archive.org/details/tribeishmaeldia00mccugoog.

The Death of Leonidas Grover

Dunn, Jacob Piatt. *Greater Indianapolis: The History, the Industries, the Institutions, and the People of a City of Homes.* Chicago: The Lewis Publishing Company, 1910, pp. 402-403.

"Hoaxes Common in Early Papers." *Indianapolis Star*, 27 September 1953, p. 2H.

"Killed by a Meteor." *Fort Wayne News and Sentinel*, 17 January 1879, p. 3.

Marimen, Mark; James A. Willis; and Troy Taylor. "The Meteor that Hit (Or Didn't Hit) Leonidas Grover." *Weird Indiana.* New York: Sterling, 2008, p. 21.

Taylor, Stephen J. "Killed by a Meteorite." *Hoosier State Chronicles*, 1 April 2015. blog.newspapers.library.in.gov/killed-by-a-meteorite.

Sidebar: "April Fool Day Jokers Active." *Indianapolis Star*, 2 April 1929, p. 12.

Cocktail Charlie

Boomhower, Ray E. "The Fatal Cocktail: Charles W. Fairbanks and Theodore Roosevelt." Ray E. Boomhower's Books, 11 May 2020, rayboomhower.blogspot.com/2020/05/the-fatal-cocktail-charles-w-fairbanks.html.

"Playing Both Sides." *Warrick Enquirer,* 19 July 1907, p. 3.

"Roosevelt Silent on the Demon Rum." *Brooklyn Daily Times*, 3 July 1907, p. 1.

Stoner, Andrew E. "Vice President 'Cocktail Charlie' Warren Fairbanks." *Wicked Indianapolis.* Charleston, SC: The History Press, 2011.

The Marketing Genius of Carl Fisher

Fisher, Jerry M. *The Pacesetter: The Untold Story of Carl G. Fisher.* Fort Bragg, California: Lost Coast Press, 1998.

The Indy Stunts of Harry Houdini

Advertisements. *Indianapolis Star*, 24 December 1907, 1 January 1908, 25 December 1911, 27 December 1911, 14 March 1915, 19 March 1915, and 29 March 1925.

"Box Made by Ayres Men Fails to Hold Houdini." *Indianapolis Star*, 1 April 1925, p. 14.

"Houdini Accepts Ayres Challenge." *Indianapolis Star*, 31 March 1925, p. 9

Lorentz, Lisa. "Sunday Adverts: Hoosierdini." *Historic Indianapolis*, 12 October 2014. historicindianapolis.com/sunday-adverts-hoosierdini.

"Magician Pulls Local Minister Out of Audience." *Indianapolis Star*, 13 October 1925, p. 2.

Mitchell, Dawn. "Retro Indy: Handcuffs, Cask Couldn't Hold Harry Houdini." *Indianapolis Star*, 13 September 2015. indystar.com/story/news/history/retroindy/2015/09/11/retro-indy-handcuffs-cask-hold-harry-houdini/72125270.

The Search for a Snake Hostess

"Five Women Wish to Act as Hostess for Gigantic Snake." *Indianapolis Star*, 1 July 1924, p. 10.

"Help Wanted—Girl to Act as Hostess at Big Shrine Party." *Indianapolis Star*, 30 June 1924, p. 3.

"Hostess Is Selected for Party on Snake's Birthday." *Indianapolis Star*, 2 July 1924, p. 10.

"Leadership Shifts in Queen Contest." *Indianapolis Star*, 3 July 1924, p. 22.

"Miss Rudd Faces Den of Snakes for Purse of Gold." *Indianapolis Star*, 6 July 1924, p. 14.

Surprising Connections

John Muir's Indy Ordeal

Colwell, Mary. *John Muir: The Scotsman Who Saved America's Wild Places.* United Kingdom: Lion Hudson, 2014.

Gisel, Bonnie Johanna. *Kindred & Related Spirits: The Letters of John Muir and Jeanne C. Carr.* Salt Lake City: University of Utah Press, 2001.

Miller, Rod. *John Muir: Magnificent Tramp.* New York: Tom Doherty Associates, 2005.

"Theodore Roosevelt and the National Park System." National Park Service. www.nps.gov/thrb/learn/historyculture/trandthenpsystem.htm.

Thomas Edison's Light Bulb Moment

Dyer, Frank Lewis, and Thomas Commerford Martin. *Edison: His Life and Inventions.* New York and London: Harper & Brothers Publishers, 1929, pp. 66-68.

Morris, Edmund. *Edison.* United States: Random House, 2019, pp. 594-595.

Actor Turned Assassin

Loux, Arthur F. *John Wilkes Booth: Day by Day.* United States of America: McFarland & Co., 2014.

The Inspiration for *Uncle Tom's Cabin*

Ashton, Susanna. "The Black Fugitive Who Inspired Uncle Tom's Cabin and the End of US Slavery." *Clemson News*, 17 July 2024. news.clemson.edu/the-black-fugitive-who-inspired-uncle-toms-cabin-and-the-end-of-us-slavery.

Brock, Jared. "The Story of Josiah Henson, the Real Inspiration for Uncle Tom's Cabin." *Smithsonian Magazine*, 16 May 2018. smithsonianmag.com/history/story-josiah-henson-real-inspiration-uncle-toms-cabin-180969094.

Dunn, Jacob Piatt. *Greater Indianapolis: The History, the Industries, the Institutions, and the People of a City of Homes. Vol. I.* Chicago: The Lewis Publishing Company, 1910, pp. 242-244.

Sidebar: "Fanny Van de Grift Stevenson." The Robert Louis Stevenson Museum. stevensonmuseum.org/robert-louis-stevenson/the-life/family/fanny-stevenson.

The *Dracula* Connection

"English Actor-Baronet Concluding Long Tour." *Indianapolis Journal*, 7 March 1904, p. 10.

"Sir Henry Irving at the Denison." *Indianapolis Journal*, 23 March 1896, p. 3.

Taylor, Stephen J. "When the Man Who Inspired Dracula Caused Blood to Boil in Gilded Age Indy." *Historic Indianapolis*, 5 October 2015. historicindianapolis.com/when-the-man-who-inspired-dracula-caused-blood-to-boil-in-gilded-age-indy.

Sidebar: Zeigler, Connie. "History 301: City Didn't Make Much of an Impression on Wilde." *Urban Times*, 5 November 2021. urbantimesonline.com/2021/11/05/history-301-city-didnt-make-much-of-an-impression-on-wilde.

A Visit from a Chinese Prince

Green, Kelsey. "Moy Kee Part II: A Royal Visit." *Untold Indiana*, 27 June 2022, blog.history.in.gov/tag/prince-pu-lun.

"Heir to Throne of China Is in Indianapolis." *Indianapolis Star*, 19 May 1904, p. 1.

"Plans for the Visit of Prince Pu Lun." *Indianapolis Star*, 5 May 1904, p. 1.

"Prince Learns Meaning of the Strenuous Life." *Indianapolis Star*, 22 May 1904, p. 1.

"Prince Sleeps While Women Await Coming." *Indianapolis Star*, 21 May 1904, p. 1.

Schoppa, R. Keith. "Visit of Chinese Prince Pu Lun." *Encyclopedia of Indianapolis*, indyencyclopedia.org/visit-of-chinese-prince-pu-lun.

"Ten Thousand See Prince at Fairview Park." *Indianapolis Star*, 23 May 1904, p. 1.

"'Very Fatigued,' Says Prince After Hard Day." *Indianapolis Star*, 20 May 1904, p. 3.

"Women with Large Feet Charm Prince." *Indianapolis Star*, 21 May 1904, p. 11.

Jim Jones, Monkey Salesman

Campbell, Don G. "Bottled Up in Customs: 'Given Up' by Church, Monkeys Are Saved 'Spiritually' Anyhow." *Indianapolis Star*, 10 April 1954, p. 1, 9.

"Two Monkeys Get New Home; Customs Office Gets $51." *Indianapolis Star*, 13 April 1954, p. 16.

The Woman Behind *I Love Lucy*

Davis, Madelyn Pugh. *Laughing with Lucy*. Cincinnati: Emmis Books, 2005.

Gilbert, Tom. "The Woman Behind Lucy's Laughs." *New York Times*, 5 August 2011.

Klink, Angie. "Madelyn Pugh Davis: Girl Writer for 'I Love Lucy'–Part 1." American Writers Museum, 23 May 2017. americanwritersmuseum.org/madelyn-pugh-davis-girl-writer-for-i-love-lucy-part-1.

Klink, Angie. "Madelyn Pugh Davis: Girl Writer for 'I Love Lucy'–Part 2." American Writers Museum. 20 July 2017. americanwritersmuseum.org/madelyn-pugh-davis-girl-writer-for-i-love-lucy-part-2.

"Madelyn Pugh Davis, Writer for 'I Love Lucy,' Dies at 90." *New York Times*, 21 April 2011.

The First, Oldest, and Largest

Union Depot and Union Station

Bilger, Nathan. "History of Indianapolis Union Station, Part 1." Historic Indianapolis, 6 May 2011, historicindianapolis.com/history-of-indianapolis-union-station-part-1.

Bilger, Nathan. "History of Indianapolis Union Station, Part Two." Historic Indianapolis, 13 May 2011, historicindianapolis.com/history-of-indianapolis-union-station-part-two.

Gadski, Mary Ellen. "Union Station." *Encyclopedia of Indianapolis*, indyencyclopedia.org/union-station.

Hetherington, James R. "The History of Union Station." Indiana Historical Society, indianahistory.org/wp-content/uploads/565f6ed967b4f468b6ba289757163a62.pdf.

Holloway, W. R. *Indianapolis: A Historical and Statistical Sketch of the Railroad City*. Indianapolis: *Indianapolis Journal* Printers, 1870, pp. 258-259, 334.

Hyman, Max R., Ed. *Hyman's Hand Book of Indianapolis*. Indianapolis: M. R. Hyman Company, 1897.

McDonald, John P. *Lost Indianapolis*. Charleston, SC: Arcadia Publishing, 2002.

The Booth Tarkington Civic Theatre

"About." Booth Tarkington Civic Theatre. civictheatre.org/about.

Klass, Michael. "Booth Tarkington Civic Theatre." *Encyclopedia of Indianapolis*, indyencyclopedia.org/booth-tarkington-civic-theatre.

Lemons, Marni. Phone interview. 17 October 2024

The Children's Museum

Children's Museum of Indianapolis, The. "The History." thehistory.childrensmuseum.org.

Kriplen, Nancy. *Keep an Eye on That Mummy: A History of The Children's Museum of Indianapolis*. Indianapolis: The Children's Museum of Indianapolis, 1982.

The International Orangutan Center

Bailey, Leslie. "Hello, Neighbors." *Indianapolis Star*, 18 May 2014, p. E1.

McCleery, Bill. "Donors Get Sneak Peek at New Orangutan Center." *Indianapolis Star*, 26 August 2013, p. B1.

"Orangutans: About." *Indianapolis Zoo*. indianapoliszoo.com/animals/orangutans.

Rudavsky, Shari. "Hall of the Wild." *Indianapolis Star*, 21 March 2014, p. 1.

"Simon Skjodt International Orangutan Center." *Indianapolis Zoo*. indianapoliszoo.com/international-orangutan-center.

Crown Hill Cemetery

Nicholas, Anna. *The Story of Crown Hill*. Indianapolis: Crown Hill Association, 1928.

Wissing, Douglas A., Marianne Tobias, Rebecca W. Dolan, and Anne Ryder. *Crown Hill: History, Spirit, Sanctuary*. Indianapolis: Indiana Historical Society Press, 2013.

Famous Locals

President Benjamin Harrison

Calhoun, Charles W. *Benjamin Harrison*. New York: Times Books, 2005.

Harrison, Benjamin. *Speeches of Benjamin Harrison*. Ed. Charles Hedges. New York: United States Book Company, 1892.

Madam C. J. Walker

Bundles, A'Lelia. *Madam Walker Theatre Center: An Indianapolis Treasure*. Charleston, SC: Arcadia Publishing, 2013.

Michals, Debra. "Madam C. J. Walker." National Women's History Museum. womenshistory.org/education-resources/biographies/madam-cj-walker.

Steve McQueen

Terrill, Marshall. *Steve McQueen: The Life and Legend of a Hollywood Icon.* Chicago: Triumph Books, 2010.

Kurt Vonnegut

Lafave, Chris. "Kurt Vonnegut." *Encyclopedia of Indianapolis.* indyencyclopedia.org/kurt-vonnegut.

Shields, Charles J. *And So It Goes: Kurt Vonnegut: A Life.* New York: Henry Holt and Company, 2011.

Oscar Robertson

Aldridge, David. "Oscar Robertson, and Indianapolis, Deserve Center Stage During NBA Showcase Weekend." *New York Times*, 18 February 2024, nytimes.com/athletic/5264188/2024/02/18/oscar-robertson-indianapolis-nba-all-star-weekend.

Flatter, Ron. "Oscar Defined the Triple-Double." ESPN.com.

"Oscar Robertson." NBA. nba.com/kings/history-oscar-robertson.

Robertson, Oscar. *The Big O: My Life, My Times, My Game.* Lincoln and London: University of Nebraska Press, 2003.

Major Taylor

Ritchie, Andrew. *Mayor Taylor: "The Fastest Bicycle Rider in the World."* San Francisco: Cycle Publishing/Van Der Plas Publications, 2010.

Oscar Charleston

Beer, Jeremy. *Oscar Charleston: The Life and Legend of Baseball's Greatest Forgotten Player.* Lincoln, Nebraska: University of Nebraska Press, 2019.

David Letterman

"David Letterman." Britannica. britannica.com/biography/David-Letterman.

Zinoman, Jason. *Letterman: The Last Giant of Late Night.* New York: HarperCollins, 2017.

Jane Pauley

"Jane Pauley." CBS News. cbsnews.com/team/jane-pauley.

Pauley, Jane. *Skywriting.* New York: Random House, 2004.

Index